WALKING IN VICTORY

WHY GOD'S LOVE CAN CHANGE YOUR LIFE
LIKE LEGALISM NEVER COULD

DENNIS McCALLUM

WALKING IN VICTORY:
WHY GOD'S LOVE CAN CHANGE YOUR LIFE
LIKE LEGALISM NEVER COULD

International Standard Book Number 978-0-9836681-5-2

New Paradigm Publishing
Columbus, OH

Dennis McCallum is Co-lead Pastor at Xenos Christian Fellowship in Columbus, Ohio, and the author of several books, including *Discovering God: Exploring the Possibilities of Faith, Organic Discipleship*, and *Members of One Another*.

CONTENTS

PART 1: GRACE

WHO ARE YOU?

In Romans 1-4 Paul provides the most in-depth and liberating discussion of spiritual birth in the New Testament. This new birth gives us a new standing with God. But spiritual growth, which comes after spiritual birth, is the essential process where the Holy Spirit changes our character. Romans 5-8 is the premiere passage in the New Testament on how to grow spiritually. At the heart of these chapters is the need to understand, believe, and apply our new identity in Christ.

The ugly parts of humanity are present in us because humans have turned away from God (Genesis 1:27; 3). Romans 5 teaches that God's answer to our problems has to do with both our old identity from Adam and our new identity "in Christ." Before we can appreciate what it means to be "in Christ," we have to come to grips with what it means to be "in Adam." Or, to put it another way, before we can experience God's yes, we have to comprehend his no.

THE URGENCY OF LEARNING

The apostle Paul begins his discussion of spiritual growth by saying, "Through one man sin entered into the world, and death through sin" (Romans 5:12). Some Christians mistakenly skip over this part, but that leads either to the despair of ongoing spiritual infancy or to something worse: Christian Phariseeism.

We can't grow spiritually by tinkering with our outward actions while leaving the inside untouched: In that we would be like a child calling to his parents to watch him swim in the wading pool, but all the while holding himself up with his hands on the bottom of the pool and furiously kicking his feet. The child, of course, is not swimming at all. He is pretending, as he mimics the actions of a swimmer. Unfortunately, this is how Christians have to live their lives when they skip over key abstract passages of scripture like Romans 5. At certain times such Christians become painfully aware they are faking it, but not sure what to do differently.

God usually makes certain that we have to enter waters too deep for this sort of phoniness. That's when we find ourselves wondering whether we missed something in the area of spiritual growth. Our formulas for success break down and we find ourselves struggling in confusion. Such times of undeniable failure could persuade us finally to come to grips with the deeper portions of New Testament teaching. Otherwise, we won't be able to move on to real maturity in our Christian lives. Instead, like the Pharisees of old, we might plod along, observing numerous spiritual disciplines, struggling to be more devoted, wringing our hands through confessions of personal sin, but all the while never really changing on the inside.

DOING AND BEING

So what does this have to do with Adam? Just this: *Our problem is not just what we do, but also what we are.* God is directing our attention to Adam in this key passage because he wants us to see how things work in the spiritual realm. Specifically, he wants us to see that *doing* arises out of *being.*

Paul writes, "Therefore, just as through one man sin entered into the world, and death through sin, and so death spread to all men, because all sinned…" (Romans 5:12). Paul is not teaching in this verse that each of us has also sinned in our turn, and so we too have to die. On the contrary, the point here is that we all sinned at the same time Adam did. This becomes clear in the rest of the passage.

In verse 17 he says, "By the transgression of the one, death reigned through the one." In other words, death reigns, not through our many individual sins, but through *one single sin.* Again in verse 18 he says, "So then as through one transgression there resulted condemnation to all men…." It's unmistakable: Paul is teaching that our problem with death and condemnation is the result of Adam's sin. That's why in verse 14 he says that the problem of sin and death also affects "those who had not sinned in the likeness of the offense of Adam." Any doubt disappears when we look at verse 19, where he again affirms that "through the one man's disobedience the many were made sinners."

Many of us have heard this teaching before. Even the Puritan Primer says, "In Adam's fall, we sinned all." But what does it mean, and what's the point for our lives today?

The point is vital and essential: *doing* arises out of *being*. You *do* what you *do* because you *are* what you *are*.

This is what the Pharisees didn't understand. Jesus criticized the Pharisees because they cleaned the outside of the cup, but not the inside (Matthew 23:25). If we focus only on changing our behaviors, we miss the real point. Instead of living out what we *are*, we define ourselves by what we *do*. According to God, this amounts to the tail wagging the dog. The point is not just that we *do* the wrong thing, but that we *are* the wrong thing!

Imagine a powerful ruler who ordered his police force to forcibly deal with his citizens' misuse of alcoholic beverages totally and permanently. They send out agents into houses, stores, and bars throughout the country to seize and destroy every bottle of beer, wine, and liquor in existence. After an intensive campaign, they successfully eliminate every drop of alcohol in the country. This illustration (borrowed from Chinese author Watchman Nee) certainly seems like a comprehensive solution. But they left something out. What did they do about the distilleries and breweries that produce the beverages? If they leave these untouched, within days millions of bottles will again flood the country.

Of course, no government would be foolish enough to carry out such a superficial program. But sadly, many Christians live their lives this way! If we want to get off the treadmill of endless reform programs that seem to go around in circles, we have to come to grips with the issue addressed in this passage: the issue of who we are, the issue of our identity. God wants us to hear something important from Romans 5 and 6: It's not enough to change what we do; we have to change who we are.

AS IN ADAM, SO IN CHRIST

According to Romans 5:12-21 we have all inherited a certain identity and nature from our ancestor, Adam. This nature involves the s-word; "sin." Though people may not want to hear it, we are sinners by nature because of Adam. Being a sinner by nature doesn't just mean I do some bad things. It means that at my very core I want sin. I'm proud, fearful, hostile, and ungrateful. This nature (along with the fallen state of the rest of the world) explains why, from the cradle up, we experience powerful negative urges.

Christian apologists are glad the Bible teaches our fall from grace because this teaching explains why evil exists. This is very different than the teachings of most religions, which see no problem with the existence of evil. In this study, however, we are not interested in apologetics, because that's not why Paul brings up our fall from grace in this passage. Rather, he wants us to see not only *what* we have inherited from Adam (our identity as sinners), but also *how* we inherited it (the principle of "federal headship"). This is the principle we must understand if we are to stop living based on what we do rather than on what we are.

FEDERAL HEADSHIP

How did we get our fallen nature? What did you or I do to end up in this state? The answer is simple: we were born. We made no decision either good or bad. From the first day of our lives, we were sinners by nature. Notice that this truth is taught in numerous other New and Old Testament passages—for example, Psalms 51:5 and Ephesians 2:1 and 3, where Paul says we "were *by nature* children of wrath."

We don't need to go into great depth about what it means to have a fallen nature right now. It's enough to say our fallen nature accounts for our tendency to rebel against God and against all authority. It causes us to desire independence in the negative sense of the word—what we could call autonomy, or self-rule. Sadly, our fallen identity also means we come into life spiritually dead, separated and alienated from God. This spiritual death is why we need a second birth to give us spiritual life and union with God (Jn. 3:1-16; Eph. 2:1-6; 2:8-10). But receiving the second birth won't necessarily change us in the deeper ways God has in mind. For that we need our spiritual birth to be followed by spiritual growth.

Our main concern at this point is *how* we got this fallen nature. Here are a few points to note, all of which will become important later in our study.

- We were not personally in the Garden of Eden.
- We did not decide to eat the forbidden fruit.
- We did not *sense* Adam eating the fruit.
- We have no tangible experience that confirms our relation to Adam as a federal head.
- Yet, if we believe the Bible as Christians, we are obligated to accept God's testimony here that our identity comes from Adam.

THAT'S NOT FAIR!

Does it seem unfair that we are negatively affected by a man's decision thousands of years ago? How do I know whether I would have made the same decision if I were there? Even if I would have made the same, wrong decision, shouldn't I get the chance to blow it on my own behalf? Why is my life being ruined by someone else's choice?

These are all good questions. Maybe an illustration will help us understand the answers.

I come from Scottish stock, and the Scots have a history of violence. Suppose my great grandpa, no doubt named McCallum, became involved in a duel over the hand of a lady. The duel was between him and another Scot named McClure, and they fired guns at one another, to the death. Who do you suppose won such a duel?

The answer is obvious. I wouldn't be writing this today if McClure had won. Great Grandpa McCallum *must* have won, because I'm here. In a sense, you could say I won this duel because I was in my Grandpa (literally) when he won the duel. Certainly if he had lost, I would have lost with him. I had no choice in the matter. I could not, and still cannot, feel this victory. Yet here I am, so he must have won the victory (if we suppose such a duel ever happened).

This illustration clearly shows that one human's choice can affect others, even though they may not agree with the choice or, for that matter, have any voice in the choices made. This must be true in many areas. Suppose someone pushed a button launching missiles for a nuclear war. Wouldn't we all be affected even though we never decided to do anything? The awesome power of free choice includes the possibility of choosing something that will result in unfairness to others.

This principle is especially true when dealing with our descendants. My choice of a wife directly affected the genetic makeup of my children, and they had no say in the matter. It's the same way with our ancestor, Adam. What this man did affected him, but it also affected his offspring. Every one of Adam's children came out the same as him: already alienated from God, already determined to do things their own way, already sinners. We are also children of Adam. Adam acted for all of us, so we never get to make our own individual choice to become rebels from God.

We are rebels by nature, not just on the outside, but from our innermost selves. When we rebel or avoid God, we are not acting only on the outside in some superficial way. We are acting out of what we truly are at the deepest level: rebels and fugitives from God. That's why we have no trouble living a consistently self-centered way of life. All we have to do is follow the course of least resistance, and we will naturally act out what we are by nature. Our *doing* arises out of our *being*.

Because Adam acted for us in this way, bestowing a certain nature and identity upon us, he is called our "federal head." If we accept this proposition, we see that having a federal head who bestows a certain identity upon us is very important, either negatively or positively. In our case with Adam, the effect is negative. But there is a ray of hope as well.

If receiving our Adam identity leads to a way of life apart from God—a way of life so easy to carry out that it's like being a fish in water—perhaps this principle can work in a positive direction as well. Anyone who has read ahead in Romans already knows this is exactly how God addressed our problems. Like Adam, Christ became a federal head.

LOSING OUR IDENTITY IN ADAM

Before anything can change on the deepest level in our lives, we have to lose the identity we got from Adam. As long as that identity remains the same, our outer actions may change to some extent, but such change doesn't amount to much in any ultimate sense.[1]

Consider our treatments for the common cold. We take nasal decongestants to reduce inflammation. We take aspirin for the headaches and pains. We may even take an antihistamine to dry up a runny nose. But one thing is clear: none of these will *cure* the cold. Such treatments only control the *symptoms* of the cold. That's because there *is* no cure for the common cold! Since we have no cure, we might as well try to control the symptoms. We have no better option.

Many Christians must have reached the same conclusion about their sin nature. They are trying to control the worst of the symptoms of their Adam-nature, but none of their measures are getting at the source of the problem. This is unfortunate, because with the Adam-nature, we do have a cure! It's a shame to see people dealing with their sin problems only on the symptomatic level when they could be experiencing real change.

---

1. Losing our identity in Adam is different than losing our sin nature, as we will explain later.

AN IMPORTANT QUALIFICATION

Before going on, we need to make one very important qualification. When we argue that trying to alter our outer behavior is like trying to control the symptoms of a cold, you might conclude that any effort to correct external behavior is Phariseeism. You might even conclude that efforts in this direction will prevent or block real change based on who you are rather than on what you do. But that would be the *wrong* conclusion.

Controlling negative behavior is not wrong, but it is insufficient. We should find ways to decrease destructive, sinful behavior in our lives and to increase positive behavior. Such behavioral control only becomes a problem when controlling our behavior is the *only* thing we know how to do. It becomes a serious problem when we begin to define our spiritual state on the basis of how well the battle with sinful behaviors is going.

The issue is not whether we attempt to control behaviors, but how we view that attempt. Do we see controlling our behaviors, or our performance, as either the *definition* of spiritual growth or the *key* to spiritual growth? If we answer "yes" to either one of these questions, we have a very serious problem, not unlike that of the Pharisees.

On the other hand, we may have certain areas of sin in our lives that need to be controlled in an external way, even though such control is not the same as spiritual growth. We need to control some particularly destructive behaviors even if by external means, so they will not block our advancement toward maturity. We might say that while controlling negative behavior is not the key to growth, it could be a pre-condition to growth in some cases.

Suppose you're an alcoholic. Your drinking and your abuse of your family are sinful and destructive. Stopping these behaviors will not make you a mature Christian, but you should seek control of the behaviors, *even through external means*, like avoiding drinking situations or even by entering a rehabilitation program. Stopping the drinking may open the door for other, more complete solutions.

The same could be true of promoting positive behaviors. Suppose you have problems being with other people. You don't like to go out in the evening, and groups of people make you nervous. In such a state, it may be very difficult to take advantage of Christian fellowship. Unless you find ways to overcome such a reluctance to act, you won't fully experience God's plan for your life.

Again, when our struggle to gain control over behavior becomes the defining issue of our lives, we've missed the point. All too easily we begin to view enhancing our external behavior as equivalent to spiritual growth. But even non-Christians change their behavior! Many Hindu and Buddhist religionists undergo disciplines much more impressive than any we are likely to practice. But is this the same as being conformed to the image of Christ? It is not.

WHAT HAPPENS TO OUR ADAM IDENTITY?

If we received our identity in Adam simply by being born, how will we ever get rid of it? The Bible is crystal clear on this point: The only possible fate for the person in Adam is death.

God will not set about renovating the Adamic person for use in the Kingdom. The verdict of death has already been decreed over this humanity. Verse 15 of Romans 5 states it plainly: "By the transgression of the one the many died." Earlier in Romans this message is repeatedly emphasized. "The wages of sin is death," proclaims Romans 6:23a, and we can rest assured, God will not change his verdict. Yet, he is able to say, "The free gift of God is eternal life in Christ Jesus our Lord" (6:23b).

We already know that Jesus bore the penalty for our sin on the cross. This explains why God can forgive us and give us eternal life. But what about the effect of his death in *this* life? How does Jesus' death affect our spiritual growth?

Here is where our study of identity in Adam begins to pay dividends. Romans 5 and 6 teach that, like Adam, Christ has become a new federal head. This is what Paul means in Romans 6:3-4:

> Or do you not know that all of us who have been baptized into
> Christ Jesus have been baptized into His death? Therefore we
> have been buried with Him through baptism into death, in order
> that as Christ was raised from the dead through the glory of the
> Father, so we too might walk in newness of life.

We saw earlier that the only way to escape the domination of the Adam nature is death. This passage mentions death in the same connection, but with a different twist. Here we discover not only that Jesus died in our place, but also that somehow we died *with* him.

This passage is teaching that God has declared us to be "in Christ," which, among other things, means we have died to what we were "in Adam." What does this saying, "in Christ," mean? We find it easy to understand a similar statement; "Christ in me." I open my heart, and Jesus enters through the Holy Spirit. But this is something completely different: not Christ in me, but me in Christ.

This is what theologians call "identification with Christ." It means God has *identified us with Jesus*. Therefore, as far as God is concerned, what is true of Jesus has become true of us. Did Jesus die? Then so did I. Did Jesus rise from the dead? Then I, too, rose from the dead.

The comparisons can be pressed even further. Did Jesus ascend to the Father in Heaven? Then according to my identification with Christ, I too ascended to Heaven and took my seat at the right hand of the Father. This is expressly stated in Ephesians 2:5-6: "And even when we were dead in our sin and transgression [God] made us alive together with Christ... and raised us up with him, and seated us with him in the heavenly places in Christ." Of course we have not become the creators of the world, nor have we become deity, but this identification with Christ goes much further than many think.

On one level, our identification with Jesus seems quite abstract. In what sense am I seated with Jesus in Heaven? In what sense am I still seated right here? How can God say I died, when I clearly am alive? Wouldn't I have noticed this experience?

USING OUR INSIGHT

We already have the key to answering these questions: federal headship. Adam was our federal head. We didn't feel or sense anything he did. We had no tangible experience of him imparting his nature to us. Yet his action directly impacted what we are. 1 Corinthians 15:45 says, "The first Adam became a living soul, the last Adam became a life giving spirit." Jesus is the last Adam. He is a second federal head. He is the last Adam because, just as Adam gave rise to a fallen humanity, Jesus became the source of a new, righteous humanity. One humanity is doomed to die; the other humanity has already died. One humanity lives in alienation from God; the other is alive to God.

Paul reiterates this in 1 Corinthians 15:21-22, where he says, "For since by a man came death, by a man also came the resurrection from the dead. For as in Adam all die, so also in Christ all shall be made alive."

BAPTISM INTO CHRIST

These statements in 1 Corinthians are just like what we see in Romans 6. According to our passage, the key to our new identity is that we have been "baptized into Christ." This is not referring to water baptism, but to spiritual baptism.

The verb baptize (Gk. *baptizo*) need not refer to a ritual involving water. Sometimes "baptize" is used for immersing people into other things. For instance, John said Jesus would baptize people in the Spirit or in fire (Matthew 3:11). Jesus asked James and John whether they were able to undergo the baptism he would undergo, referring to his suffering and death (Mark 10:38). The exact meaning of baptism must be determined in each passage by considering the context. The word means "immersion" or a "putting into." But immersion into what?

Here in Romans 6 Paul is not commenting on our immersion into water, but into Jesus himself. This is the baptism by the Spirit. Paul says this "baptism," or immersion into Christ, is an integral part of becoming a Christian. He often refers to God's act of placing believers into Christ. In 1 Corinthians 12:13 he says, "By one Spirit we were all baptized into one body." This is why believers are called the Body of Christ. In 1 Corinthians 1:30 Paul says, "By God's doing you are in Christ Jesus." The Spirit of God has somehow baptized, or placed us into Christ.[2]

Theologians refer to this joining us to Jesus as the "mystical union" of believers with Christ. The New Testament refers to believers over 100 times with expressions like "in Christ," "in the beloved," "in him," or similar phrases. The mystical union of the believer with Christ is far from being an obscure concept found off in some theological corner of the Bible. Many of the most important promises God gives us are linked directly to this union. Here are some important examples:

---

2. Some Pentecostal theology argues for a baptism of the Holy Spirit that comes later in the Christian life, as a second act of God. Here we are not referring to any second act of grace. Rather, the New Testament is clear that this identification with Jesus happens to all believers at the moment of conversion, as all the verses in the chart below demonstrate.

Things We Received Based on our Identification With Christ

PASSAGES	WHAT IS PROMISED
ROMANS 8:1 There is therefore now no condemnation for those who are in Christ Jesus.	Freedom from condemnation
ROMANS 8:2 For the law of the Spirit of life in Christ Jesus has set you free from the law of sin and of death.	Freedom from the law of sin
ROMANS 8:39 [Neither] height, nor depth, nor any other created thing, shall be able to separate us from the love of God, which is in Christ Jesus our Lord.	Security and permanence in God's love
ROMANS 12:5 So we, who are many, are one body in Christ, and individually members one of another.	Unity with other Christians
1 CORINTHIANS 1:5 In everything you were enriched in Him, in all speech and all knowledge.	Spiritual gifts
1 CORINTHIANS 1:30 But by His doing you are in Christ Jesus, who became to us wisdom from God, and righteousness and sanctification, and redemption.	God's wisdom, goodness, etc. imparted to us

2 CORINTHIANS 2:14

But thanks be to God, who always leads us in His triumph in Christ, and manifests through us the sweet aroma of the knowledge of Him in every place.

Triumph or victory in spiritual war

2 CORINTHIANS 5:17

Therefore if any man is in Christ, he is a new creature; the old things passed away; behold, new things have come.

New identity

GALATIANS 2:20

I have been crucified with Christ; and it is no longer I who live, but Christ lives in me; and the life which I now live in the flesh I live by faith in the Son of God, who loved me, and delivered Himself up for me.

Death to the old person

GALATIANS 3:28

There is neither Jew nor Greek, there is neither slave nor free man, there is neither male nor female; for you are all one in Christ Jesus.

Basis for social, racial, and gender equality before God

EPHESIANS 1:3

Blessed be the God and Father of our Lord Jesus Christ, who has blessed us with every spiritual blessing in the heavenly places in Christ.

Every blessing, note the past tense

PHILIPPIANS 3:9
[That I] may be found in Him, not having
a righteousness of my own derived from
the Law, but that which is through faith in
Christ, the righteousness which comes from
God on the basis of faith.

Righteousness
imparted to us

PHILIPPIANS 4:7
And the peace of God, which surpasses all
comprehension, shall guard your hearts and
your minds in Christ Jesus.

Inner peace

COLOSSIANS 3:3-4
For you have died and your life is hidden with
Christ in God. When Christ, who is our life,
is revealed, then you also will be revealed with
Him in glory.

Future inheritance and
eternal life

I JOHN 5:20
And we know that the Son of God has come,
and has given us understanding, in order that
we might know Him who is true, and we are
in Him who is true, in His Son Jesus Christ.
This is the true God and eternal life.

Truth and understanding

2 CORINTHIANS 5:21
He made Him who knew no sin to be sin
on our behalf, that we might become the
righteousness of God in Him.

The righteousness
of God

When we analyze the promises in these and other passages, we find one over-arching theme: What is true of Christ is also true of us who are in Christ. Jesus is victorious; therefore, we are led in his victory. Jesus is at the right hand of God; therefore, we are also. According to Romans 6, death and resur-rection are two of the most important things true of us once we are in Christ.

GOD'S VIEWPOINT

Considering the promises attached directly to it, this teaching must be very important. It may help to consider the problem from God's viewpoint.

As already stated, God's verdict on the Adam nature is final. We will never experience freedom from our fallen nature until we die and are resurrected in a new body. What might God do in the meantime? He could solve the problem by striking all who receive Christ dead immediately and taking them to Heaven right there and then. This solution has some clear drawbacks. If everyone who believed in Christ immediately fell dead, Christian evangelism would become harder than it already is! Besides, who would do the witnessing?

Whether for these reasons or others, God went a different direction. Instead of striking all believers dead, he has judicially *declared* them dead by identifying them with Christ. This means God chooses to view us as we are in Christ; that is, he views us the same way he views his son. This sounds incredible. Our standing before God couldn't be higher. But is it real, or is this just double talk? How can I have died and been seated in Heaven when I'm clearly sitting right here, seemingly the same as ever?

First, who views us as being "the righteousness of God"? I know I find it very hard to view myself that way. My wife finds it even harder! It is not my wife or me, but God who views me this way. But this doesn't mean our identification with Christ is just a dream in the mind of God. Our status is quite real. Consider the fact that one day our fallen existence will end, either when we die or when the Lord returns. However, our standing in Christ will never end or change. When we think of it this way, our standing in Jesus is even more "real" than our life in Adam.

Second, the fact that we have been identified with Christ is an issue of faith for Christians. 1 Corinthians 1:30 says, "By God's doing you are in Christ." That is a plain proposition that we might not fully understand, but that we need to accept as a declaration from God. We don't need to be able to confirm this statement with some kind of experience or feeling. It's a fact of scripture that deserves willing belief from those of us who view scripture as our ultimate standard of truth. The truest thing about us is what God says about us.

Remember, we did not sense or feel anything of Adam's fall, yet we received a fallen nature because he was our federal head. People could give other explanations for why we have a selfish nature. The reason we as Christians believe our problems came from Adam is not that our experience tells us so, but because God has declared this to us in his word.

God also declares that we who trust in Christ have died and risen with him, though we cannot feel this truth either. Therefore, we have the same reason for believing in our identification with Christ as in our identification with Adam: God tells us so.

Finally, when we consider our sense of identity, we realize that how God looks at us is not an unimportant abstraction. This idea is so important, and it comes up so often in the study to follow, that we will devote a whole chapter to understand it better.

IDENTITY: WHAT IS IT, AND HOW DO WE PERCEIVE IT?

When you look in the mirror, who looks back? "That's me!" you say. As humans, we have a stable experience of a real self.

But our total sense of identity involves more than this. We also assign various areas of positive and negative value to ourselves. For instance, some of us might say "That's me, the car dealer," or, "That's me, the musician." If we thought about it longer, we might add, "That's me, the wife of so-and-so," or "That's me, the son of so-and-so." Then we might have some other value judgments: "That's me, the one with the big nose," or, "That's me, the fat one." With each element that comes to mind, we expand and complete our total sense of identity. Of course, many of us would include the observation, "That's me, the Christian."

Interestingly, not everything we have done or every feature of our bodies, life histories, or mental makeup would come to mind even if we thought about it for a long time. Some things just don't figure into our consideration of who we are. For instance, we might not ever bother to point out, "That's me, the one with a filling in my twelve-year molar." We may have such a filling, and in that sense it is as much a part of the total description of who we are as the size of our nose, yet we don't view it as a significant part of our identity. Why? Such a feature may be real and measurable, but for some reason it just doesn't matter. Why do I consider some things important, and therefore a part of the definition of my identity, while I view others as insignificant?

The usual answer is that some things have become important because of what other people say and think. We usually draw our sense of identity from others' views of us. The following illustration should help us understand how our sense of identity develops.

A LONELY NIGHTMARE

Suppose nothing existed in the universe except you.

There you are, floating in a bubble in the midst of infinite, empty space. What would your identity be? What would you consider important? Suppose you asked yourself, "Would I be considered tall or short?"

"Hmmm," you say. "Tall or short compared to what?" Ideas like tall and short come from comparisons with others. But nothing and no one exits in this imaginary universe but you. Would you consider yourself smart or stupid? Here again, such concepts are directly dependent on perceptions of yourself *relative to others*. If you were the only one in the universe, they would be meaningless. And so it would go in every area. Whether you considered your activities, traits, or anything else, you would have no way to assign importance to anything. Consequently, you would have no sense of identity. You could only wonder who you were and whether you mattered. You could never know anything about your identity with any real meaning or confidence.

This nightmare is designed to illustrate a point. Your sense of identity depends on definitions and values that originate outside yourself. Unless you can relate aspects of yourself to some external reference point, all your views are arbitrary and pointless. Things like meaning, value, and importance only make sense when viewed in the context of a larger picture.

Suppose in your lonely universe, another person comes floating up in his own bubble.

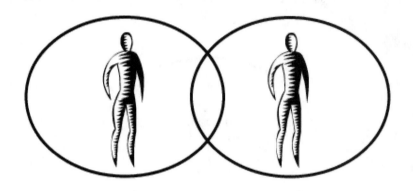

At least now you have someone to compare yourself to. We could call him an *external reference point*, because he isn't inside your head. You might notice you are taller than him and conclude that, therefore, you are a tall person. However, for all you know, this other person might be the littlest person ever, and you aren't very tall after all. Since both of you are floating in a sea of infinite nothingness, your comparisons would all be questionable in terms of whether they reflect anything important. You might notice that you have five fingers, but the other person in the universe has six. Is this important, or just a curiosity? There's no way to tell.

With two, you now have an external point of reference—a reference point outside yourself. The problem is, this external reference point is *finite*, or limited, just like you are. You have no reason to think his features mean anything more than yours did before he came. So having two of you really doesn't answer any questions. You still have no way to tell what the real story is. Any conclusion you draw about yourself could just be a comment on the other person. In such a universe, everything is relative; nothing would be definite in the area of values.

For your identity to be fixed and real, you have to be able to relate your features to some infinite or absolute reference point outside yourself.

Apart from God, the human race is living in this dilemma, and non-theistic thinkers are increasingly realizing it. Instead of one other person to compare ourselves with, they point out, we have millions. This means we can begin to establish sociological averages, but those don't really tell us anything either.

You might find that, on average, you would be considered obese. This could be discouraging, especially if everyone around you thought fat people were ugly or bad. Interestingly, in some poor countries today, being fat is a sign of wealth and is admired accordingly. Which view is right? We might say, "I'll decide what I think about that for myself." But probably the real truth is that we will answer according to the view of other people around us.

A WORLD ADRIFT

When we consider our world, we realize that while we may not be individuals floating alone in space without meaning, our whole planet is floating in space; so what's the difference? All the people on our planet are busy comparing themselves to each other, trying to decide which comparisons are important and which ones are not. But if we can't relate our judgments to any absolute perspective, they are all quite arbitrary. In a real sense, such judgments are just as meaningless as the judgments you might arrive at in your solitary bubble.

Of course, this is not how people usually look at things. mhm We begin as children and our parents tell us what's important. They impart a lasting sense that some things about us are good and others are bad. Our sense of what is important is our values system. good or bad

Later in life, our friends' opinions may come to have more importance than those of our parents. We may then modify part of the values system we received from our families based on our friends' influence. Generally, by the time we are adults, we have formed opinions about what matters and what doesn't, and we have formed some sense of our own identity. Yet apart from God, we have no way of knowing whether any of these views are correct in any final way. For all we know (and in fact, it's a pretty good bet) we just happened to grow up around people who view things a certain way, and therefore we view things that same way. It's no wonder many of us feel shaky about our sense of identity.

What if there were an absolute or ultimate ruler by which we could measure things—an infinite ground on which we could stand?

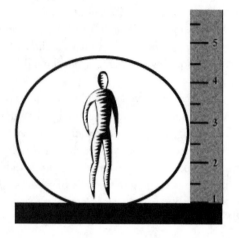

According to the biblical view, there is such an absolute. God is an external reference point, but he is different from the finite reference point in our earlier illustration. Because he is infinite and unlimited, he is also universal, or absolute, rather than relative. Other things can be related to God, but he doesn't need to relate himself to anyone or anything to know who he is. God introduced himself with the saying, "I am who I am" (Ex. 3:14). That is the beginning point for all truth and reality.

With God as our reference point, we now have an *external, infinite reference point*. Such a reference point can tell us the way things are in the ultimate sense. It's no longer a matter of how some things are relative to some other finite things.

If you believe the Bible, you should realize that God's view of us is the true view. If he views us a certain way, then that is, in the ultimate sense, the way we really are! Even if the majority of our peers look at things a different way, we would know they were wrong by referring to the infinite external reference point—the God and creator of all. Not only could we know that the view of our peers was wrong in some cases, we could even discover that *our own view is wrong as well*. If we have come to view things a certain way, but God declares they are another way, we need to change our minds.

MODERN SOLUTIONS

Modern thinkers are increasingly aware of the importance of what they like to call our "self-image." In the terminology we are using here, our self-image is our understanding of our identity, of who and what we are. These modern thinkers are referring to some of the same things Paul discusses in Romans 5 and 6, but their way of working with the idea is faulty. Modern teachers of self-image therapy urge us to shore up our shaky sense of identity in one of two ways, neither of which is successful.

Some self-image theorists call for pure, abstract self-affirmation. One TV comedy had a nerdy guy Steward Smally, who would look in the mirror and say, "I'm good enough, I'm smart enough, and gosh darn it, people like me!" This satire referred to an actual school of thinking seen in self help literature in our culture. You're supposed to repeat to yourself how good and valuable you are, in the belief that this will heal your sense of inadequacy and self-hate. But like the earlier person in a bubble, you have no objective reason to believe any of these statements. The TV comedy where Stewart Smally looks in the mirror and tells himself he's okay, pokes fun at those foolish enough to think that merely saying so makes it true.

The concepts of "good" and "value" in themselves have no objective meaning without reference to a personal creator God. We can tell ourselves anything we want, but when we have no reason to believe our statements are true, our words will have a hollow ring. Any effect they have on our sense of self will be temporary at best.

Other modern thinkers, including even some Christian thinkers, argue that the key to a good self-image lies in hanging around with affirming people who will say you are important. This solution is hardly surprising coming from secular thinkers, who base their understanding of personal identity and values on the views of others. It is quite odd, however, and even bizarre to hear such solutions from Christians, who should know we that cannot base our identity on what other people think.

Other people's views and attitudes constantly change, and they are often false. If we base our identity on what others think, we become the playthings of public opinion; we become man-pleasers, dependent on others' views of us for our sense of well-being or identity.

A DIFFERENT SOLUTION

According to scripture, this is not God's way. As Christians, we don't depend on a vote by our affinity group in order to know who we are. We are not a group of bubbles floating in space, basing our understanding on comparisons with each other. We stand on the ground of God's unchangeable character, and his infallible view of us in his son.

This is why Paul says in 2 Corinthians 10:12, "When [people] measure themselves by themselves, and compare themselves with themselves, they are without understanding." Paul understood what modern secular thinkers and even some modern Christian thinkers have not understood. We either determine our meaning and value by referring to God, our infinite external reference point, or we base our meaning and value on the shifting relative evaluations of others.

We need to know who we are and why we matter, and God answers these questions in the Bible. According to him, when I was a non-Christian, I was in Adam, and my identity was that of a sinner. Now, I have a new identity in Christ. We're ready to return to Romans.

KNOWING, BELIEVING, CONSIDERING

We left the book of Romans at the point where God said we who are "in Christ" have been united with him in his death and his resurrection from the dead. This means our identity in Adam has ceased, and we now have a new identity. We are part of a new humanity in Christ. This language can sound terribly abstract when we first read it. Even after years of study, some struggle at times with feelings that this teaching is not real. It may be good to re-read the passage, and we have included it here if you wish to do so:

> Or do you not know that all of us who have been baptized into Christ Jesus have been baptized into His death? Therefore we have been buried with Him through baptism into death, in order that as Christ was raised from the dead through the glory of the Father, so we too might walk in newness of life. For if we have become united with Him in the likeness of His death, certainly we shall be also in the likeness of His resurrection, knowing this, that our old self was crucified with Him, that our body of sin might be rendered powerless, that we should no longer be slaves to sin; for he who has died is freed from sin. Now if we have died with Christ, we believe that we shall also live with Him, knowing that Christ, having been raised from the dead, is never to die

again; death no longer is master over Him. For the death that
He died, He died to sin, once for all; but the life that He lives,
He lives to God. (Romans 6:3-10)

According to this passage, the key to gaining victory over sin is our new
identity. First, what does God say I am? Then, do I believe it? Or, How do
I see myself? These questions are not the same. I may view myself as something very different than what I actually am. We don't agree with modern
secular teaching on self-image. To the secular thinker, the important thing
is that I think highly of myself. If I think I'm cool and wonderful, then I am.
Whatever I think I am, that's what I am.

According to the Bible, what matters most is what I *actually am*. Only
when I know the answer to this question can I exercise faith and use
my mind to *experience* what I am. In modern thinking, my mind shapes
reality. Under the biblical model, God shapes reality and my mind needs to
understand and appropriate what God has done.

I could easily be one thing, but view myself as something different. We are
subjective beings. We view ourselves a certain way, and that may or may not
be in accordance with reality. As a result, the fact that we have a new identity
in Christ may be having little effect in our daily experience. If so, we are
missing the freedom promised in this passage.

KNOWING

In Romans 6:1-10 Paul several times refers to our *knowing* the facts regard-
ing our mystical union with Christ. In verse 3 he says, "Or do you not *know*
that all of us who have been baptized into Christ Jesus have been baptized
into his death?" Again in verse 6 he says, "*Knowing* that…" And finally, in
verse 9 he again says, "*Knowing* that…"

Three times in these few verses Paul seems to be challenging us about
what we know, or should know, about our new identity in Christ. Knowing
the facts is crucial to our ability to move forward. Let's review the facts in
verses 1-10 in Romans 6 quickly before going on.

ONLY THE FACTS PLEASE!

First, as we saw earlier, all Christians have been united with Christ through
spiritual baptism. This is the act of God whereby he places us into the Body
of Christ. He says "we were all" baptized in this way, which means this

unification with Christ is true of every Christian, not just the few or the elite. This past-completed tense means we need do nothing to accomplish this unification. It is an historic fact. *alive again.*

Paul says our union with Jesus means that we died and rose with him. He's not saying that each of us had a discreet death and resurrection event. Rather, there was only one death and resurrection—Jesus' 2000 year ago. Our discreet event is our placement into Jesus. Then, his death and resurrection became ours.

Now we have served our death sentence, which means our old identity—the persons we were in Adam—have died *vicariously* through Christ. We are rid of our old self.

We have also risen with Christ, which, according to Paul, means that we can now walk in a "newness of life" that includes freedom from sin. We also have a new intimacy with God. The absolutely righteous creator God views us as having the same standing before him as his own son. *Crazy. insane.*

This is the way God views us. And as we saw earlier, the way God views us is our true identity. But something could be true of us with little effect if we don't know about it.

A story is told of a prospector in Nevada who worked a claim on the eastern slopes of the Sierra Nevada range. He never found much gold in the stream, so he lived a poor life in a shack. When he died, some of his prospector buddies found him and buried him on his own claim, in front of his shack. While digging the grave, they hit a strange bluish clay that struck one of prospectors as strange. He took it to a lab to be assayed, and it turned out to be a rich silver ore. It was the tip of a huge deposit later known as the Comstock Load—the biggest silver find in U. S. history.

If this story were true, this old man had the mineral rights to the Comstock Load. He was the richest man in the world! But it never affected his life because he didn't know about the ore. So we see that knowing what's true about you can be just as important as the facts when it comes to the effect on your life.

AN IMPORTANT DISTINCTION

Please notice an important distinction as you read Romans 6:6. Paul says, "Knowing this, that our old selves were crucified with Him *that our body of sin might be done away with*, that we should no longer be slaves to sin." This statement, found in both the *New American Standard Version* and the *New International Version*, is a misleading and mistaken translation.

Our "old self," which was crucified with Christ, and our "body of sin" are not the same thing. The term "body of sin" refers to our *sin nature*, inherited from Adam, whereas the "old self" refers to our *identity* in Adam. These are related, but different.

My old self is the person I was before receiving my new identity in Christ. That old self has been crucified—he exists no longer as far as God is concerned. This is why God says, "If any man is in Christ, he is a new creature; the old things passed away; behold, new things have come" (2 Corinthians 5:17). This is my new identity.

My body of sin, on the other hand, is the nature I also received from Adam. That sin nature is still there; it has not been "done away with," as verse 6 says in these versions. This should be obvious. How could I think my sin nature has been done away with when I regularly experience temptation?

This translation of the verse, first found in the King James Version has badly wounded many sincere Christians. They concluded that this verse is teaching perfectionism (not unreasonably considering the translation). Perfectionism is the notion that we can become sinless in this life. But John warns us, "anyone who says he is without sin is a liar and the truth is not in him" (1 John 1:10). The Bible never teaches perfectionism.

In truth, our sin nature is still alive, but if we apprehend our new identity in Christ, this sinful nature can be *rendered powerless*. This is how the Greek word *katargethe* should be translated. The *New American Standard Version* gives this reading in the margin as an alternative. I think it should be in the text as the preferred reading. A quick check with a concordance or lexicon will show that its primary meaning is "to render powerless," or "to nullify." It can mean "to destroy" or to "put an end to," but that doesn't make sense in this context. Paul is talking about freedom from slavery, which requires that our sin nature be rendering powerless, not removed altogether.

Paul is explaining the key to breaking our sin nature's power over us. We break the sin nature's power by properly understanding and applying our new identity. Verse six is saying that we have a new identity (the old man was crucified) so that our sin nature will be rendered powerless—that is, we are no longer slaves to sin.

So, we don't need to pretend we no longer have a sin nature. That solution would be closer to the notion of 'mind power,' where we create reality through what we think. In this passage Paul is only asking us to recognize the truth. Appropriating this truth can break the sickening power of our sin nature to a substantial degree. God is not promising sinless perfection here; he is offering an opportunity for *relative* victory over sin.

BELIEVING

These are the facts. God doesn't see us in Adam any more. He now sees us in Christ, as new creatures, perfectly acceptable to him, and welcome into even the most intimate union and fellowship with God. The big question is: Do I believe this passage of scripture? Or are these just empty words on a page?

Something can be true of you, but never has much effect on your life for the simple reason that you don't believe it.

In a similar passage in 1 John 4:16 John says, "And we have come to know and have believed the love which God has for us." Later, he is able to say, "We love because he first loved us" (verse 19). When you view these verses in sequence, you see that we must first come to know and to believe the truth about God's view of us before the change (our ability to love at a new level) comes.

Thus we learn that something can be true about you, but never have effect in your life because you don't believe it.

Suppose a guy knocked on the door and when you answered he handed you a plastic folder. He explains that you had a rich great uncle in Europe who was unknown to you. He has recently died and left you several million dollars in a Swiss bank account. This plastic folder has checks and information on your new account. After telling him you're not interested and closing the door, you look at the folder. Knowing things like this don't happen, you quickly recognize a hoax and throw it into the trash can.

But guess what. This isn't a hoax. For the rest of your life, you own a Swiss bank account with millions in it. But you never take out any money so it never changes the way you live. You knew someone offered you a bank account with millions in it, but you didn't believe it was real.

This could happen in your spiritual life. God says one thing about you, but if you believe something else, it won't have the intended effect. As we probe further into the meaning of this passage, ask God to reveal the reality of these truths in your heart. If you're like most, you will feel a real struggle as unbelief and confusion battle with biblical faith.

CONSIDERING

Knowing the facts isn't enough. We also have to apply active faith. Real faith in the biblical sense always has an action component. According to the Bible, you haven't really believed something until you act on it. *hm.*

Verse 11 of Romans 6 says, "Even so consider yourselves to be dead to sin, but alive to God in Christ Jesus." Here is the first word of command in this passage. Until now, God already accomplished everything in the passage for us. But here, Paul calls on us to do something in response—to consider ourselves in a certain way.

The death and resurrection we have in Christ is a death to sin and a new sense in which we are alive to God. It's referring to how God views us. But how do we view ourselves? Are we relating to God and others as those who are new creatures, as those who have this new identity? Or are we relating as though we were still in our old identity? According to this verse, God wants us to deliberately view ourselves the way he views us. We are to consider ourselves to be what God says we are.

This is a conscious act of thought and will, usually associated with prayer. Before God we need to speak words of faith, agreeing with his declaration that we are in Christ, and therefore dead to sin and alive to God. That may seem very abstract and unreal, but we can ask for an "opening of the eyes of our hearts" to see what God is saying here (Eph. 1:18). As we practice seeing ourselves as God says we are, we should gain a growing sense of the reality of what we are reading.

PRESENTING

Part of deciding to believe God's clear statements about our new identity, is that we present ourselves to him accordingly. Look closely at the language in the following two verses:

> Therefore do not let sin reign in your mortal body that you should obey its lusts, and do not go on presenting the members of your body to sin as instruments of unrighteousness; but present yourselves to God as those alive from the dead, and your members as instruments of righteousness to God.
> (Romans 6:12-13)

Here, instead of saying "reckon yourselves such and so," he says "present your-selves to God as such and so." We know what it means to present ourselves to God: we should pray, and in our heart we should offer ourselves to God as his followers. That much is easy.

The interesting question is, why did he add the phrase "as those alive from the dead?" What is the difference between merely offering ourselves to God, versus offering ourselves to God *as those alive from the dead?* The difference is huge. It really is the difference between approaching God "in Adam" versus approaching him "in Christ."

Here we have the key to applying Jesus' federal headship to our lives.

THE GIGANTIC DIFFERENCE

The sad fact is that too often we approach God, not as those alive from the dead, but as those in Adam. We often come before God strongly conscious of sins we have committed and of our lack of faithfulness. We might even cower before God, depressed about how unworthy we are to approach him. Especially after failing in the same area for the umpteenth time this week, it can be pretty difficult to saunter up to God and feel like we have complete intimacy with him.

This is why God calls believers to exercise active faith. We easily come before the Lord with thanksgiving and openness when we are in the flush of victory. But so much of the time we must approach him in pain and failure. At such times, are we able to enter into his presence with the same ease and intimacy? If we are honest, we probably often have to admit that we cannot. Why? Because we are unable to see ourselves as he sees us. Instead, we are seeing ourselves based on our performance. This is a form of legalism that stifles true spirituality.

COMING TO GOD IN ADAM

When my son was young he had trouble communicating when he got into trouble or did poorly with his school work. Instead of sitting down with me for a good session of commiseration and exploration into the causes of the trouble, he would be sullen and withdrawn. As his father, it hurt when I tried to discuss it with him and sensed how he felt ashamed to talk with me about his problem. He seemed unable to find words much of the time and wanted to cut the discussion short—looking down and shuffling—even trying to slowly walk out of the room in the middle of the conversation! Sometimes he lied to avoid having me find out about a failure. It was frustrating to realize he didn't grasp how I viewed him.

This must be similar to the way God feels when we skulk up to him, reluctantly spending some time in prayer and wringing our hands fitfully the whole time. When we come this way we are presenting ourselves to God as those still in Adam, not as those alive from the dead. We are coming to God in our old identity rather than our new one. If we are honest, many of us will have to admit this is the way we approach God much of the time. *Ya. so tru 4.*

No wonder God calls on us to "consider (or reckon) ourselves dead to sin but alive to God in Christ Jesus." Our tendency to view ourselves as though we were still in Adam could break down our intimacy with God and rob our Christian walks of life and freedom. We need to look much closer at what it means to consider ourselves in our new identity.

Dann mgh.

CONSIDERING OURSELVES: THE SPECIFICS

Paul exhorted the Roman Christians; "In the same way, count yourselves dead to sin but alive to God in Christ Jesus" (Romans 6:11).

Some Bible teaching stresses Paul's call in this passage to consider ourselves dead to sin. This view argues that Paul calls on the believer to reckon himself dead to sin each time temptation arises. Thus, it is argued, he will find deliverance because if you're dead to something, you can't continue in it. However, the argument becomes vague at this point. The bottom line is that the battle against sin consists mainly of trying to convince myself that I'm dead to sin, even though I still desire it.

I used to find this teaching quite confusing as a young Christian. If you've tried to deal with burning temptation by telling yourself "I'm dead to this," you know what I mean. It doesn't work all that well. In fact, it doesn't work at all. I always got the feeling I was trying to think my way into something that wasn't quite true in the first place. I sure didn't feel very dead!

But the verse doesn't teach that we are dead. We are obviously not dead. The real point of the verse is not just that we are dead to sin but that *we are alive to God!* So we are alive, not dead. We were alienated from God in Adam. Sin and death reigned over us. In Christ, we see ourselves *not* enslaved to sin, *not* alienated from God, but *alive* to God. We are treasured in his eyes. We are welcome into the deepest level of intimacy with him because we are in Christ.

Only when we begin to see ourselves this way and consistently approach God accordingly will we experience the power promised in this passage. Only then will we:

- Begin to escape the performance fixation that leaves so many believers defeated and broken in their own self-effort.
- Realize the freedom and power of a perspective that is truly Christ-centered.
- Gain regular, increasing freedom from our sin habits.
- Be delivered from love demanding, self-pity, and selfish ingratitude.
- Enter into a new level of praising and worshiping God.

How vital it is that we come to the place where, like Paul, we can say, "The life I now live, I live by faith in the Son of God" (Galatians 2:20).

RELATING OUR CONSIDERING TO PROBLEMS WITH SIN

Romans 6:12 ties together the notion of viewing ourselves in Christ on the one hand with freedom from sin on the other hand when it says, "Do not let sin reign in your mortal body." How does this relationship work?

First, this passage is not teaching that any time we adopt the right view of ourselves we won't sin. Paul isn't referring to the *impossibility* of sin, but to the *incongruity* of sin as a way of life for those who are alive to God in Christ. Seeing ourselves in Christ leads to seeing a jarring discontinuity between our new lives and sin. When we continue in sin, it creates a tension between what we are and what we are doing.

The relationship between gaining freedom from sin and seeing ourselves in Christ is not mechanistic. We can't repeat some formula when we feel tempted and expect that to end the temptation (contrary to what some teachings on this passage seem to suggest). God is explaining in this passage how we should relate to him and to ourselves on the basis of who we are, not giving us magic words that put an end to temptation.

In the longer view, those who exercise faith in God's statements about their new identity will have more victory over sin in their lives with each passing year. Those who fail to do so will automatically fall under a works perspective that leads to fakery, or to giving up.

FREEDOM AND LAW

Our choice is spelled out for us in Romans 6:14: "For sin shall not be master over you, for you are not under law, but under grace."

The implication of this passage is clear: If we *were* under law, sin *would* be master over us. But why bring up the issue of law and grace in the context of how we consider ourselves? Because of the issue with which we began our study—*doing* versus *being*.

If you seek victory over sin merely by focusing on your behavior, you are under a performance perspective that amounts to legalism.[1] Under the legalistic perspective, altering our behavior is what matters. Legalistic thinkers believe that changing what we do means we are changing what we are. Legalism is usually linked to a shallow view of sin that allows people to believe that human willpower can eliminate most sin. Legalists have to overlook ninety percent of what constitutes sin in order to make it seem like avoiding sin is possible. But the irony is that legalistic thinking actually leads to *more* sin, not less (as Paul states in Rom. 6:14).

If you let yourself come under law, you'll think your identity and blessing depends on your performance. Contrary to what we read in Romans 6, where being in Christ gives you your identity, you'll come to believe that avoiding sin gives us you your identity. You'll think that by not sinning, you're not a sinner, even though that's never possible. Legalistic teachers even use the statements in Romans 6 to threaten believers. They argue, "It says right here that if you continue in sin, you are not in Christ."

Legalism. Don't go there. It spells defeat of the most sickening kind. The Pharisees were legalists, and Jesus saved his harshest words for them.

Grace means that God supplies the power for change. Under grace, God has already granted blessing and identity, and as I apprehend that fact, I will be transformed by it—not always as much as I should be, but way more than I would be under legalism. This is why Paul teaches that we can only experience freedom from sin when we're under grace. This truth flies in the face of those preachers and authors who beat the drum for righteous living based on a fear-threat motive. According to verse 14, such shrill teaching will only result in further bondage to sin.

---

1. Legalism technically means the teaching that one is justified by Law. The technical term for the belief that one must grow spiritually by law is "nomism." But in popular speech, legalism applies to both views, so I use it in its popular sense here.

INDIRECT CHANGE

Look at the language of verse 13: "Do not go on presenting the members of your body to sin as instruments of unrighteousness; but present yourselves to God as those alive from the dead, and your members as instruments of righteousness to God."

Why does Paul use such cumbersome language? Instead of "do not go on presenting the members of your body to sin as instruments of unrighteousness," wouldn't it be easier to say, "Don't be unrighteous?" Doesn't Paul know about succinct writing? At the end of the verse comes a similarly verbose phrase: "[Present] your members as instruments of righteousness to God." Here again, why not just say, "Be righteous" or, "Do good?"

This cumbersome language is not a mistake. Paul carefully chose this phraseology to communicate a certain message and to avoid giving the wrong impression. We must see the difference between "doing good" and "presenting ourselves as instruments of goodness." The first formula implies that I can simply decide to good on my own. The second implies that I don't have that power; all I can do is present myself to God as his instrument for goodness. He is the one who needs to bring out goodness in me. This is an essential recognition: I must access God's power through his grace, because I am helpless in myself to change.

So, Paul's wording is an example of the cautious approach of one who understands the relationship between the believer's will and victory over sin. This relationship is an *indirect* one. We do use our will. We need to present ourselves to God a certain way in order to grow spiritually. But if you think you have the ability to turn away from sin in yourself, you are trying to use self to change self, and it won't work.

Rather than calling on believers to set their minds on law-living, this verse calls on us to set our minds on God—who we are in Christ. The result is a Christ focus rather than a sin focus.

HOW IT WORKS

Again, we are not arguing that Christians need not use our wills. In fact, using our power of choice is essential. But we are not directing our wills toward ourselves, simply ordering change of performance. Instead, we actively come forward to depend on God, who then uses his power to change us. We have to come to him with the right perspective—that we are alive from the dead in Christ—and this usually entails a period of reflection and review. We might put it this way: We use our wills, with the right attitude and mindset, to present ourselves to God, who then uses his power to change us.

As we cultivate this mindset over a period of time, we will notice gradual change in our characters. The time here is measured in months and years, not hours and days. Living out of our new identity by faith releases the Holy Spirit to empower us.

The difference between the direct and indirect approaches to character change can be confusing. It's certainly not as simple as it sounds. Ironically, we may understand the theory behind this passage at one point in time, only to realize that we are again and again arrogantly seeking to bypass God in our quest for good works and character change.

"BEING" APPLIED TO "DOING"

In Romans 6:17-19 we have a restatement of this principle in very clear terms:

> But thanks be to God that though you were slaves of sin, you became obedient from the heart to that form of teaching to which you were committed, and having been freed from sin, you became slaves of righteousness. I am speaking in human terms because of the weakness of your flesh. For just as you presented your members as slaves to impurity and to lawlessness, resulting in further lawlessness, so now present your members as slaves to righteousness, resulting in sanctification.

The following diagram may help us understand this language. Paul first refers to their past conversion.

You were slaves of sin	You became slaves of righteousness

This is a simple statement of what has already occurred. God moved us from our identity as slaves of sin in Adam to a new identity—that of slaves of righteousness in Christ. Notice the past tense. This already happened.

Now comes another row with an imperative, a word of direction, based on that past fact:

You were slaves of sin	You became slaves of righteousness
You presented your members as slaves of impurity	Now present your members as slaves of righteousness

The bottom row represents verse 19. God is saying, "When you *were* slaves of sin you presented yourselves as slaves of impurity" (the left column). Nothing could be more reasonable than that. How else would a slave of sin present himself?

When unconverted, we acted as what we were: sinners. Our intent and focus was not on how to avoid sin or to do righteousness, but on how to enjoy sin and preserve our freedom to sin. So box one and three belong together.

Now we have moved from box 1 to box 2. What should be the result? Obviously, now that we *are* slaves of righteousness, we should take the view of slaves of righteousness and present ourselves accordingly. But often we don't. It is sadly possible to move from box 1 to box 2 but not to move from box 3 to box 4. When this happens, we are living out of our old identity. We are failing to acknowledge our new identity or to present ourselves in it.

Suppose I have a friend who is a criminal. He is sentenced to twenty years in prison for various crimes and serves the time in one of the harshest dungeons ever. In his stone cell he keeps track of the days by scratching lines on the wall. He even has to use a bucket in the corner as his toilet.

After twenty years, I pick him up at the prison and insist that he come to my house while he adjusts to freedom. At home, things don't go as expected. He rarely leaves the guest room, and before long I notice a smell coming from inside. Finally, I stop by and ask to come in. As he lets me into the room I'm horrified to see that he has been scratching lines on my freshly painted wall, and has even soiled my trash can!

What would you say in this situation? I know what I would say: "Hey pal, haven't you overlooked something? You're not in prison anymore!"

That's just what Paul is saying in this passage. "You used to do these things when you were a prisoner because you had no alternative. You *can* still do them; it's *possible* to do these things even though you're now free. But how incongruous! How unbefitting!" It's clear that my friend still sees himself as a prisoner.

I could get heavy with him, threatening expulsion from the house, but this would be off target. I want him to stop his antisocial behavior (especially the bit with the trash can), but there's more involved here than his behavior. He clearly doesn't realize his freedom. What a shame it would be if he changed his behavior because I threatened him, but never changed his outlook.

God wants us to understand what he has done to our identity. He wants us to experience this change increasingly in our lives, not through gritting our teeth in fleshly self-effort based on fear of rejection, but through the power of his transforming love.

POSITION VERSUS CONDITION

		Position
You were slaves of sin	You became slaves of righteousness	
		Condition
You presented your members as slaves of impurity	Now present your members as slaves of righteousness	

In this version of the chart you see labels on the right hand side for each row—*Position* and *Condition*. Our *position* refers to what is judicially true of us in Christ. Our position in Christ is unchanging, perfect acceptance and imputed righteousness. Ephesians 2:6 says that God has "seated us with Him in the heavenly places in Christ Jesus."

Our *condition* refers to our daily experience, which can vary as we experience well-being and adversity, spiritual health, and sickness. One day our condition may be that we are abiding in Christ and enjoying our closeness with him. On another day we may be fleeing from God and falling into sin. One day we feel victorious. The next we feel defeated. Although we have some control over our condition, it also includes circumstances beyond our control.

The point of this passage is that God wants us to view ourselves the way he views us—in our *position*. When we see ourselves as we are in our *position*, it leads to victory. This is what Paul means when he says we should present ourselves to God as those alive from the dead. Christians who develop this position-focus gain victory for two reasons. First, our faith in God's word releases the power of the Holy Spirit to conform us to our position. Second, a position-focus exerts a gentle inner pressure to change. The sheer incongruity between how we behave when we sin and our new identity causes us no longer to feel comfortable in sin. The joys of sin seem pointless and bizarre, losing their appeal.

Conversely, viewing ourselves in our *condition* leads to defeat. In our condition, we have no way to define ourselves other than our performance and our feelings. The resulting works focus will lead to bondage, as Paul warned in Romans 6:14. Condition-focused people also lack gratitude, often feeling sorry for themselves because their circumstances are problematic. They are constantly taking their emotional temperature and are rarely satisfied with what they find.

GOD'S PERSPECTIVE VERSUS HUMAN PERSPECTIVE

		Position
You were slaves of sin	You became slaves of righteousness	God's perspective
		Condition
You presented your members as slaves of impurity	Now present your members as slaves of righteousness	Human perspective

The next set of boxes above and below the center line in the diagram contain the words *God's perspective* and *Human perspective*. God always views us in our position. That's why he can accept and love such imperfect people. We, on the other hand, are prone to view ourselves and others in our condition. To us, the truths of scripture are often not as real as our experiences, our circumstances, and our feelings.

At times it becomes strikingly clear that the truth of our position in Christ means little to us, as signaled by the lack of gratitude in our hearts. Any time we feel sorry for ourselves, we must be seeing ourselves in our condition, not in our position. Our prayers also reflect this condition focus. We fret and whine about our situations and our feelings. We may have little or nothing to say to God about our position in Christ.

Again, God wants us to begin viewing ourselves the way he views us. By including this passage and many others like it in the New Testament, God shows us how to develop a position focus.

INDICATIVE VERSUS IMPERATIVE

		Position
You were slaves of sin	You became slaves of righteousness	
		God's perspective
		Indicative
		Condition
You presented your members as slaves of impurity	Now present your members as slaves of righteousness	Human perspective
		Imperative

The final pair of terms in the diagram is *Indicative* and *Imperative*. In grammar, we can either say how things *are* or how they *should be*. When we describe the way things are, we use the *indicative* mood. When we say how things should be, like when we issue a command, we use the *imperative* mood.

When scripture teaches, "By God's doing you are in Christ Jesus," it makes an indicative statement. It tells us the way things already are. When Paul says, "Therefore, reckon yourselves dead to sin but alive to God in Christ Jesus," he is making an imperative statement—a statement of command. It tells us what we are supposed to do.

We see both indicative and imperative statements in scripture, but the important thing is the *relationship between* these two, especially in the New Testament. You see the pattern clearly in Romans 5 and 6. The imperatives, or commands, are always based on the indicative statements describing what God has done. In other words, what we are supposed to do is always based on what God has already done.[2]

---

2. We have focused on the past-tense indicative here, but indicatives also apply

This may sound like a lot of theological mumbo-jumbo, but it's vitally important for every Christian. The relationship between the indicative (what God has done or is going to do) and the imperative (what I am supposed to do) gets at the heart of two important components of our motives.

In the first place, because my instructions are based on what God has already done, I obey not *in order* to gain my standing with God, but because *I already have* a right standing with God. The difference here is profound. Ask yourself, "Am I trying to give God a reason to bless me? If you answer "yes" to this question, you are functioning under law, where blessing depends on performance.

If you are responding to the fact that God already has blessed you, you are correctly motivated; you are basing your actions (imperatives) on God's indicatives. You are not trying to earn anything. You realize who you are. Unlike my prisoner friend, you realize that that you are no longer a prisoner, and you are responding accordingly. It's fascinating and liberating to see this relationship unfold in one passage after another throughout the New Testament. You can see a few choice examples in Appendix 1.

Seeing the imperative as depending on the indicative separates the Pharisaic Christian from what we might call the *resting* Christian. A resting Christian is one who depends on God's power for character change and who is secure in his or her acceptance during the process.

Some teachings today put so much emphasis on the imperatives of scripture that readers lose touch with all importance of Scriptural indicatives. It's not that they deny the great statements about God's acts on our behalf. Instead, the importance of such statements becomes unclear. Constantly banging away at the imperatives of scripture without carefully covering and reviewing the *basis* for such commands (the gracious gifts of God) creates a legalistic tone, very far from what we read in passages like Romans 5 through 8. Even though legalistic teachers can quote imperative verses that seem to support their view, they have lost the larger picture.

Perhaps an example will help. Suppose your dad gave you a brand new car for your birthday. As he hands you the keys, he says, "There are two things I want you to know about this car. First, this car is a free gift from me to you. Second, it's going to cost you $10,000."

---

to the present or the future. For instance, God says He will give us an inheritance in eternity future. This is an indicative statement that serves as a basis for numerous imperative statements, such as those urging us to "lay up for [ourselves] treasures in heaven" (Matthew 6:30).

Obviously, whatever the first statement means, it becomes incomprehensible when the second statement cancels it out. Ownership of the car is apparently conditional, so why talk about a free gift? Likewise, when law-oriented teachers bang away at imperatives endlessly, we forget what the indicatives mean and why they are important.

What if your father took a different approach? Suppose as he handed you the keys he said, "This car is a free gift from me to you, and because of that, I hope you'll respond to my generosity by using it responsibly." This is a very different model from the first example, and closer to what God is saying in this passage. Ownership of the car does not depend on our using it responsibly. To the contrary, our responsible use of the car depends on our ownership. It is precisely *because* we were given a generous gift that we are being asked to do something.

THE BIG PICTURE

In your hands you hold this book. Suppose the book could speak to you, and it said this: "I know I have fallen short, and I'm sorry. I want to change but I don't feel able. I know what I need to be, but I am not. Please give me the ability... give me the grace and the power to become... a book."

I would have to say, "Okay, hold it right there. You already are a book!" This silly illustration must be similar to what God feels when we completely ignore our identity in Christ and insist on relating to him as though we were still in Adam.

Let's consider it a different way. How much effort do you expend trying to avoid wetting your pants or shaking a rattle? I know I don't spend any energy at all trying to avoid these things. They are activities I used to do, and I probably even enjoyed doing them. But these days, I have no particular urge to engage in this kind of activity. I did those things when I was a baby. Now, it just wouldn't be appropriate, because I'm an adult. I *could* still do these things. That's certainly possible. But it would be incongruous and ridiculous.

There may have even been a transition period when I struggled to change my ways. But eventually, I accepted that I wasn't a baby any more, and I turned away from such activities for good. By turning away from these infantile behaviors, I am acting based on what I am: an adult. For that reason, it causes little or no strain for me to behave this way.

Unfortunately, changing our character won't be as easy as learning to go to the bathroom. Learning to change in non-moral and external ways is easy. Nothing in my nature insists on wetting my pants. Changing from autonomy to God-centered, sacrificial love will grate on me quite a bit more, but the principle for change will be similar.

Imagine how frustrating and confusing it would be to strive to enter a room you're already in! It's no different when we struggle to become someone we already are in Christ. We need to begin turning away from who we were in Adam and accept who we are in Christ. We need to begin to "consider ourselves dead to sin and alive to God in Christ Jesus."

How wonderful to realize that God has acted on my behalf—independently, irrevocably, and lovingly! He has given me a new identity in Christ. When this indicative, what the author of Hebrews calls this "finished work," breaks in on me fully, my relationship with God will be revolutionized. Rather than moan in defeat, I will sing words of praise.

LAW SCHOOL

The notion of acting on the basis of our identity in Christ is such a beautiful concept, but somehow it just isn't complete. You may be reading this discussion, shaking your head, and saying to yourself, "It isn't that easy. I've heard something like this before, but it doesn't work."

Too often, our efforts to reckon ourselves alive to God in Christ seem to make little difference, especially in the short run. This is not a magical state of mind that precludes failure. Rather, this mindset is the *backdrop* for the dramatic but gradual measures God will take in our spiritual growth. We have an inherited nature tending toward sin, pride, and autonomy, as well as years or even decades of trusting that nature to run our lives. That means fundamental change won't come easily. Included in the process are numerous painful lessons in what we could call "law school."

A RADICAL, EXTREME PASSAGE

Romans 7:1-6 is one of the most extreme and startling passages in the Bible. Why not read it carefully right now?

> Or do you not know, brethren (for I am speaking to those
> who know the law), that the law has jurisdiction over a person as
> long as he lives? For the married woman is bound by law to her
> husband while he is living; but if her husband dies, she is released
> from the law concerning the husband. So then if, while her
> husband is living, she is joined to another man, she shall be called
> an adulteress; but if her husband dies, she is free from the law, so
> that she is not an adulteress, though she is joined to another man.
> Therefore, my brethren, you also were made to die to the Law
> through the body of Christ, that you might be joined to another,
> to Him who was raised from the dead, that we might bear fruit
> for God. For while we were in the flesh, the sinful passions,
> which were aroused by the Law, were at work in the members
> of our body to bear fruit for death. But now we have been
> released from the Law, having died to that by which we were
> bound, so that we serve in newness of the Spirit and not in
> oldness of the letter.

Divorce laws have changed a lot since Paul's day, but the legal principle he cites has not. The law only has jurisdiction over someone while that person is alive. Marriage law doesn't apply to the dead, and widows are free to remarry. This analogy points to our freedom from the law.

Like most analogies, if we press it too far there are inconsistencies. For instance, here, the woman apparently refers to us. We are bound to a demanding husband who is impossible to please: the Law of God. To be perfectly consistent, the husband should die before the woman is free, but that would mean the Law of God dies, which is not possible. So, the one who dies in the analogy is actually the woman herself—that is, us. Death severs the bonds of law. Because we have died with Christ, we have moved beyond the reach of the Law.

Just as death severs the bonds of civil law, it also severs the jurisdiction of the Law of God that Moses brought down from Mt. Sinai. The Law only has jurisdiction over us while we live. Since God views us as having died with Christ, where does this leave us with regard to the Law of God? Paul clearly gives us our answer in verse 6: The law no longer has jurisdiction over us!

Some Christians are startled as this naked truth offends their senses. A tightening in the throat may already be compelling some to reach for concordances and commentaries, finding passages that show why one shouldn't take this text too literally. Within minutes, they can relax again, secure in the knowledge that the wheels aren't coming off and that, if you understand the larger picture, we are still under law after all. This passage applies to someone or something else. It surely doesn't mean the Law of God has no jurisdiction over me!

But let's hold on for a minute and give this section of inspired scripture a chance. We can go to our books later if we still feel the need. For right now, ask yourself, "Why does God say, 'Therefore, my brethren, you also were made to die to the Law?' Why does he say, 'But now we have been released from the Law, having died to that by which we were bound?'"

Notwithstanding commentators who have resisted this concept for centuries, the radical truth is right before us. We are no longer under law!

Paul says we died to the law "so that we serve in newness of the Spirit and not in oldness of the letter." What is the "letter" we do *not* serve in, and exactly what is the change Paul is calling for? As we take up the answers to these questions, we might as well also examine a parallel passage in 2 Corinthians 3 which includes some language almost identical to that in Romans 7:

> Our adequacy is from God, who also made us adequate as
> servants of a new covenant, not of the letter, but of the Spirit;
> for the letter kills, but the Spirit gives life. But if the ministry of
> death, in letters engraved on stones, came with glory, so that the
> sons of Israel could not look intently at the face of Moses because
> of the glory of his face, fading as it was, how shall the ministry of
> the Spirit fail to be even more with glory? (2 Corinthians 3:5b-8)

Here as in Romans 7, the legal code Moses brought down from the mountain is called the "ministry of death," and Paul says we no longer serve that covenant.

How urgent it is for Christians to clarify the exact meaning of these and similar passages in the New Testament. They both sound like an outright repudiation of the Law as the governing authority over Christians. But theologians have consistently advanced arguments explaining why these passages don't mean what they seem to be saying.[1]

I relegated a discussion of this debate to the footnotes for ease of reading, but not because the debate is unimportant. Christians need to study this question and arrive at a firm conclusion about what these passages mean. For now, we accept (contrary to many theologians) that such passages do indeed teach that Christians are not under law as a rule of life. God's law is still an accurate reflection of his character, and as such it has an important revelatory role. However, looking to the law for help in living the Christian life is a mistake, according to the New Testament, and will actually harm your spiritual growth.

Those who believe that Christians are still under law for spiritual growth have raised some good questions. "How can we be released from the Law of God? Has God's moral character changed?" To understand the answers to such questions, we need to understand God's reasons for giving the Law. Only then will we be able to view the Law correctly while avoiding legalism.

WHY THE LAW? DEFINING SIN

Surely right is right and wrong is wrong for all people, isn't it? Yes. And the Law explains good and evil. The principles found in the moral portions of the Old Testament Law still define wrong and right, as they always have. But the believer under grace needs to look at the Law not for detailed instructions on living, but for a general picture of what God's character is like.

---

1. A critical question for all interpreters is, "What is the difference between believers under the New Covenant and the Old Covenant?" Bible believing theologians of all schools agree that something important happened at Pentecost. This coming of the Spirit, which was still in the future in Jesus' day (John 7:38-39), resulted in the change Paul mentions in these two passages. But what, exactly changed? In what sense are we no longer servants of the letter?

Some have suggested that Christians are no longer under law for salvation, but that is impossible. Paul is clear that nobody has ever been justified by works of law, including in Old Testament times (Romans 4; Galatians 2:16). Others claim that we are released from Old Testament ceremonial law (like the sacrificial system). This is true, but the examples cited here in Romans 7 ("You shall not covet") and in 2 Corinthians 3 ("engraved on stones" = the ten commmandments) are not referring to ceremonial law, but moral law.

So again, in what sense are we released from the law in this passage? Only one possibility remains: we have been released from the law for *spiritual growth*.

This 'principlized' application of the Law can be seen in Paul's statement that "the whole Law is summed up in the saying, 'Love your neighbor as yourself'" (Romans 13:9). This is a non-legalistic analysis. No legalist would feel comfortable with a statement like this, because it is too general and leaves too much freedom. Even though Paul includes details, like not committing adultery and not stealing, it still leaves far too much to the imagination. As we shall see, details are important for legalists. Paul refers to this defining role of the law in Romans 7:7:

> What shall we say then? Is the Law sin? May it never be! On the contrary, I would not have come to know sin except through the Law; for I would not have known about coveting if the Law had not said, 'You shall not covet.'

As a non-Christian, I might feel that lusting was all right, but once I read and believe the Bible, I realize it's wrong. Now the question is, what am I to do with that knowledge? This is what separates the legalist from the non-legalist. The legalistic approach is to find the appropriate law for a given situation and apply it strictly. "Just do it!" summarizes this approach. The key is simple obedience. Stop making excuses and do what God commands!

While grace-oriented Christians also want to obey, they realize that something is missing in this picture. Is it really that easy to overcome sin in all its forms? No, it isn't, and Romans 7 makes this clear. Instead, under what Paul calls "the covenant of the Spirit," we look beneath the letter of the law to learn the great ethical principles that illustrate God's character. Then we look to the power of God to apply those principles, doing for us what we cannot do for ourselves. The grace-oriented believer realizes that simply doing the things in the law is not possible, and even if it were, it would be insufficient. We need growth that comes from within, drawing on the power of God, not just outward compliance to a legal code.

To embrace the moral teaching of the law without falling "under law" we must view the law in a non-legalistic way. The law is still there, but we are no longer *under* it. Focusing on a list of rules or orienting my thinking around rules will not help me live the Christian life. As we see in Romans, God wants us to direct our attention toward building our relationship with him, not toward the law or our failure to keep it.

When I look at my mirror these days, it shows me that I'm beginning to sag in the middle. But while my mirror can show me the problem, it does nothing to help me change. I can poke, twist and pose, but the sag is still there. The mirror is not designed to do anything about that. Likewise, the law lets me know where I'm falling short, but it can do nothing to help me change. In this sense, the law plays a similar role before and after conversion. Just as the law shows the non-Christian that he falls short of God's standards and needs grace, it shows us as Christians that we still need ongoing grace from God. But here is a strange thing: Law not only shows us we are committing sin. It also provokes us to sin *more*!

WHY THE LAW? PROVOKING SIN

Non-Christians are actually provoked to sin more when their flesh nature reacts to God's law. Paul refers to this in Romans 7:5, where he says, "While we were in the flesh, the sinful passions, which were aroused by the Law were at work in the members of our body to bear fruit for death." The law not only *exposes* our passions, it also *arouses* them, according to this verse.

A story is told of a new hotel built on a small cliff overhanging the Pacific Ocean. As it neared completion, the management saw that the second floor balconies hung over the water in a way that might result in guests trying to fish from the balcony. They were worried about liability problems, and they thought the heavy fishing weights might break the expensive picture windows behind the fishermen. So, they decided just before opening week to post signs in each room forbidding fishing from the balcony.

During the hotel's opening week, several windows were damaged by fishing gear. At a management meeting, they discussed further sanctions. Should they fine those who fished? Should they turn them out of the hotel? One smart manager suggested that before enacting draconian measures, they should try taking the signs down. They did, and they never had another incident. Whether or not this story is true, we all know the lure of forbidden fruit. The fact that something is prohibited makes it more appealing to our fallen nature.

Paul describes this effect of the Law in verse 8 of Romans 7: "But sin, taking opportunity through the commandment, produced in me coveting of every kind; for apart from the Law sin is dead."

What a strange saying, and how poorly it fits with legalistic theology! Again, according to this verse, the law does more than just define sin. It also stimulates the sin nature and produces more sin, even in Christians.[2] He goes so far as to say that "apart from the Law, sin is dead." This verse also implies that coming out from under law is part of the key to breaking the power of sin in our lives. How similar this statement is to Romans 6:14, which we already saw: "Sin shall not be master over you, for you are not under law, but under grace."

In both of these statements, the implication is the opposite of what legalistic teachers would have us believe. Far from suggesting that the Law might help us live for God, these verses say the Law encourages rebellion and sin. Other passages teach the same thing, like 1 Corinthians 15:56, which says, "The power of death is sin, and the power of sin is the law." One of the most startling verses on this subject is in Romans 5:20: "And the Law came in that the transgression might increase; but where sin increased, grace abounded

---

2. Many interpreters argue that this is not about the effect of the law on believers, but on non-believers. Their argument is mainly theoretical, not exegetical. They feel that a Christian wouldn't have the kind of reaction Paul describes here; he would just obey. By relegating this passage to pre-Christian experience, these interpreters blunt the force of Paul's teaching, allowing them to argue that Christians are still under the law as a rule of life. But this argument is wrong for four reasons:

1. Paul says, "I was once alive apart from the Law; but when the commandment came, sin became alive and I died." This statement could never refer to a non-Christian experience. In Paul's theology of human nature, we are born already in sin (Romans 5; Ephesians 2:1-6). He would never say he was alive before coming to faith in Jesus.

2. Paul would never say he delighted in the Law of God as a non-Christian (vs. 20). Paul would never say a non-Christian who sins is "not practicing what [he] wants to do but doing the very thing he hates" (verse15). Paul has already declared that with non-Christians, "there is none righteous, not even one… there is none who seeks for God." The idea of a non-Christian who hates sin and longs to serve God is incompatible with Paul's theology of human nature.

3. When Paul refers to his "inner man" delighting in God and a different flesh nature compelling him to sin (vss. 22-23) it becomes clear he is describing an experience he had as a Christian. This dual, inner/outer man language is exclusively used to describe regenerate Christians.

4. The context in Romans prohibits understanding chapter 7 as referring to the role of the law in conversion. Paul already dealt fully with this subject in chapters 1-4, and then moved on to questions of spiritual growth in chapter 5 and 6. Why would he return to discuss conversion again only to again discuss spiritual growth in chapter 8? This fatal violation of thought-flow is clear in spite of Paul's brief mention of conversion in 7:5 and 8:9, as we will see.

all the more." Does it seem strange that the law was designed to *increase* sin?
Most people think the law came to decrease sin. But this says the opposite.

YOU'VE GOT TO BE KIDDING!

So we could see the need for him.

Why would God give a law that stimulates sin? Certainly, he is not pleased
when people sin. Yet, according to these passages, he provided a law that he
knew would stimulate sin. You can probably guess the answer. God didn't
give the Law because he thought it would be obeyed. Neither did he need a
mirror with which to see our sin; he already knows all about our sin. In fact,
we are the ones who are confused. *We* are the ones who need the Law to serve
as a "tutor to lead us to Christ" (Galatians 3:24). The law convinces us that
nothing less than the free gift of God will save us.

That's fine for non-Christians, but what about Christians? Why would
God provide a law to stimulate Christians' sin natures? Essentially, the purpose is the same. Although we now realize we cannot save ourselves by good
works, we may secretly believe (or we may have been taught) that we are able
to follow God in our own strength. *hm.*

Even if we say, "Yes, I know I'm unable to change myself," God may detect
a lingering confidence in the self. He will "smoke out" this confidence by allowing us to tangle with his Law just as Paul does in Romans 7:14-24.

As Christians, some of us tiptoe over the line in smaller ways, but we
are all still thrilled on some level by violating the law. That's what it means
to have a fallen nature. That nature is not gone just because we have a new
standing in Christ. However, if we understand our new identity, we can rob
the sin nature of its awesome power over us. And understanding our new
identity includes realizing that we are no longer under law.

HOW DOES IT WORK?

In verses 9-11 of Romans 7 Paul says:

> I was once alive apart from the Law; but when the command-
> ment came, sin became alive, and I died; and this commandment,
> which was to result in life, proved to result in death for me; for
> sin, taking opportunity through the commandment, deceived me,
> and through it killed me.

In this passage Paul is discussing an experience he had as a Christian.
Certainly he would never suggest that he was once "alive" before his conversion, any more than he would claim he was not under law before conversion.
On the contrary, this time when he was "alive apart from the Law" refers
to that period *after* conversion when he felt the joy of the Lord intensely,
though he had not truly confronted his own flesh.

God usually waits for a period of time (differing in length for each of
us) before he lets us come face to face with our full impotence before the
law. In this experience we feel a sickening pull toward sin. We know God
has changed us on some level. For instance, some of our attitudes may have
changed early on with little struggle on our part. But then it turns out the
change is only temporary or nonexistent. This is especially true when we confront inner problems—attitudes, relational problems, apathy, lust, or anything
that goes beyond the external.

Some Christians report that they were delivered from addiction to drugs
on the day they received Christ. That was not my experience, but I believe
God can and does do such things. God has ample power to miraculously
deliver us from sin in a moment of time. When he elects to do so, we should
accept such blessings with joy. But even if God does give a miraculous deliverance in an area or two, he will not deliver us from our overall slavery to sin
that way. We may only be healed in one or two of the most destructive areas,
while the bulk of our growth still lies ahead.

Then we enter law school. As we strive to obey God, we fail. Then we try
harder and fail again. Shock, confusion, and even doubt may well up as the
full horror of the sin nature dawns on us. This is a dangerous period, especially if nobody ever warned us it was coming. Hopefully we won't take the

deadly turn toward legalistic dishonesty at this point. The most terrible and
destructive reaction we can have in the face of moral failure is to claim we
aren't really failing, or to claim it isn't that bad. It's just as disastrous to claim
that our failure was someone else's fault.

All of these reactions suggest the same thing: We are trying to deny our
deficiency before the Law of God. We are guarding against admitting our
inadequacy. Whether by rationalizing, minimizing, or blame-shifting, we are
refusing to learn the lesson God wants us to learn. These sin-denying tools
are the stock-in-trade of the Pharisaic Christian. They can only prolong and
worsen a treatment that cannot be avoided.

We feel torn. On one level we want to obey God, and it's difficult to
understand why we still feel compelled to sin. This is how Paul puts it in
Romans 7:12-13:

> So then, the Law is holy, and the commandment is holy and
> righteous and good. Therefore did that which is good become
> a cause of death for me? May it never be! Rather it was sin, in
> order that it might be shown to be sin by effecting my death
> through that which is good, that through the commandment sin
> might become utterly sinful.

Here Paul warns us not to blame our problems on the Law. The Law is flaw-
less, and is operating perfectly. The problem is our sin nature and its rebellious reaction to the Law. The Law is merely bringing to light the reality
and the power of that nature. This is what Paul means when he says that "sin
might become utterly sinful." When sin has "become utterly sinful," we are in
a position to admit the true extent of our helplessness.

As young believers, we often think Christians are doing well when they *avoid* sin. After some years of this treatment, we learn Christians are doing well when they *admit* sin. Paul comes to this point explicitly in chapter 7 verses 18 and 19:

> For I know that nothing good dwells in me, that is, in my flesh;
> for the wishing is present in me, but the doing of the good is not.
> For the good that I wish, I do not do; but I practice the very evil
> that I do not wish. Relatable.

What despair and pain there is in this cry! Have you ever felt this? I know I have. One could wonder whether Paul is losing his Christian walk. Is he on the verge of backsliding all the way to Hell? Far from it. This is the cry of one who is learning exactly what God wants him to learn.

He is coming to own the prerequisite to further depth with God by coming to the end of himself. He is realizing in a new way that he will never satisfy the righteous demands of God. He is also discovering that only helpless clinging to God in complete dependence holds any hope for real progress. Listen to the misery in Paul's words as he seems to reach a crisis of failure in verse 24: "Wretched man that I am! Who will set me free from the body of this death?" Yes.

Yet there is this sudden note of victory as well. "Thanks be to God through Jesus Christ our Lord!" (v. 25). Like life springing out of death, Paul finds that dependence on Jesus begins at precisely the point where dependence on self ends. The Law has done its job for the moment.

THE BATTLE OF SPIRIT AND FLESH

It's not enough that we may have felt the same sense of despair Paul does in this passage. We also need to understand what it means. Why do we sometimes feel such despair, and why does God allow it?

Earlier we pointed out that both the Old and the New Testament contain imperatives, or instructions. We should do certain things, and avoid other things. For instance, I should pray, read my Bible, and share my faith when I get the chance. But I should avoid needlessly hurting other people or becoming dependent on drugs.

As Christians, in our hearts we want to comply with these instructions. However, our old natures—what Paul calls "the flesh," want to disobey these same instructions. This often creates an inner struggle that can be quite painful. In Galatians 5:17 Paul describes this struggle this way: "For the flesh sets its desire against the Spirit, and the Spirit against the flesh; for these are in opposition to one another, so that you may not do the things that you please."

As we focus on this struggle and intensify our efforts to see the Spirit triumph over the flesh, we grow more and more frustrated every time we fail. Some Christians even resort to various forms of self-punishment and personal vows in order to gain victory. But once we utter a vow, whether verbally or mentally, failure becomes even more likely. We have now created a new law with even more authority and therefore more power to stimulate the flesh.

We could work ourselves up into a frenzy of self-effort during these episodes, sometimes at the urging of legalistic friends and teachers. But what is the result? We sin again. We fail. Even when we succeed, we lose the joy of what we are doing because our motives center in the law. We are now "under law," and as God warned in Romans 6:14, sin will be master over us until we correct the problem.

Where do we turn? I am certainly not going to suggest that we shouldn't read our Bibles or pray, or that we might as well go ahead and get drunk. But if neither the law nor wanton sin is the answer, where are we to turn? We are wretched creatures, aren't we?

People turn one of three directions in this situation, but only one of these alternatives leads to victory.

THE FIRST RESPONSE TO FAILURE: GIVING UP

Young Christians often give up during this experience. So many thousands come to Christ when they are students or young adults, but they lose their way and no longer walk with the Lord. Why does this happen so often? There is more than one reason, but I think legalism in the face of personal failure is more common than any other.

When young Christians fall into sin of some sort and are also under law, they are unable to appropriate the grace of God. They are ashamed to face God and other Christians because they know they are guilty. They feel that what they have done is so bad that God and others would reject them if they were open about it. Terrifying sermons on the consequences of sin and books that threaten sinners with every sort of doom strengthen the impression that it's not safe to fail.

While they may be right about other people rejecting them, they are wrong when they think God would do so. Right at this point Paul fearlessly declares, "There is now no condemnation for those who are in Christ Jesus" (Romans 8:1). But Satan, the Accuser of the Brethren will bore in on the sinful Christian with the idea that God couldn't be too happy to see him after the way he's been living.

Before long, all joy disappears from his walk with the Lord, and Christianity itself becomes too burdensome to bear. In sorrow, the young believer wanders away from Christian fellowship and tries to drown disappointment in some distraction. Christian leaders and older Christians must learn to recognize when young Christians are coming under this sort of performance bondage and be prepared to help deliver them from it.

THE SECOND RESPONSE TO FAILURE: LEGALISTIC DISHONESTY

Some Christians turn a different direction when caught between the demands of God's law and personal failure. They begin to distort reality in such a way that they can avoid looking at their problems. *Souls like someikaw*

Some develop a secret life that they live right alongside the public one. Publicly, they fearlessly denounce sin and wickedness. But privately, they may harbor bitterness or have some secret immoral sex from time to time. Pastors who work with outreach ministries have all met fundamentalists with dual-lives. People like this (usually from a legalistic religious background) fiercely attack sin in others, sometimes fixating on even very minor infractions. Later, however, it turns out these very self-righteous ones are involved in the most flagrant, though secret, personal sin. The entire country has been treated to this spectacle during the past few years, as several famous, angry, sin-denouncing preachers have been discovered in gross perversion and even crime.

Hypocrisy is nothing new, but no one in Jesus' day was criticized more for it than the Pharisees. Ironically, no group in all of Israel was more radically committed to obeying the law than they were. Paul himself had been one. At one time, he thought that when it came to "righteousness which is in the Law" he was "found blameless" (Philippians 3:6). How could he have lost it so badly by the time he wrote Romans 7?

Of course, he didn't lose anything. No doubt he, like other Pharisees, had an elaborate work-around for pretending to follow the law. Now, as a Christian, he had to face the law honestly. Anyone who honestly considers what it means to "love the Lord your God with all your heart, all your soul, and all your mind," (Matthew 22:37) could hardly think he was without sin for even a day, let alone his whole life!

One of the worst ruses used by legalistic thinkers is what Jesus called "straining out the gnat and swallowing the camel." In this exercise, legalistic fakers bluster furiously at frivolous external sin in order to keep everyone's attention on the easy part of the law. They don't want people to look at the inward parts of the law where they are failing miserably. In fact, the more self-righteous a person is, the more we can guarantee that person is a deceiver.

Jesus revealed that the Pharisees weren't keeping the external laws (like tithing) *along with* what he called the weightier portions of the law. Rather, they were keeping the easy laws (the gnat) *instead of* the weightier portions (the camel). When people strain out the gnat and swallow the camel, it's a sure sign that they are focusing on law rather than grace. This practice is a product of training and modeling. Legalists don't exactly realize they are straining out the gnat. Indeed, they are often the last to comprehend what they are doing.

Under a grace perspective, we can look directly into the heart of even the most demanding portions of God's law—portions that call for a life lived fully for God in real love. We can safely look at the full demands of God's law only when we have given up trying to deny we fail to keep it.

When I was growing up, we had a lawn mower that had no switch to turn it off. After using the mower, we would usually take a hammer (wood-handled was best) and lay the head of the hammer on the block of the engine so that it touched the tip of the spark plug. The result was instantaneous—the engine stopped as soon as the power to the spark plug was diverted to the block.

Similarly, our spiritual growth may be progressing in a healthy way until the day we turn to legalistic dishonesty. That wrong turn will stifle true growth just about as quickly as the hammer head stopped that old mower. We may see continued learning, minor outward change and even periodic success in Christian ministry. But we are not growing closer to God until we change our perspective. Instead, we have developed a controversy with God that we need to resolve before we can go on.

THE THIRD RESPONSE TO FAILURE: WALKING ACCORDING TO THE SPIRIT

We have seen that under the pressure of failure to keep the law, some give up while others take up the techniques of deception and hypocrisy, leading to Phariseeism. But there is a third path. This last reaction, the correct one, is "walking according to the Spirit." That will be the subject of our study in Romans 8.

LIFE UNDER LAW OR UNDER GRACE

Before continuing our study of Romans, we should make sure we understand the difference between the perspective of one who is "under law" and one who is "under grace." If it seems we are pounding this issue hard, that's because abundant evidence shows that contemporary Christians have great difficulty understanding the difference between these two perspectives. Legalism is a subjective state of mind, and therefore is hard to describe in objective terms. We can easily fail to recognize the earmarks of legalism in our own lives.

Remember, it's not that the law isn't there any more, but that we are not *under it.* The law hasn't been done away with, but our relationship to it has changed.

One way to understand being under law is that I am basing my identity on my performance. Under law, I draw my view of what I am from what I do. Days of success make me feel proud and happy. Days of failure make me feel like Paul in Romans 7. But the main point is that I am not growing in grace as long as I live under this perspective. That's because when I am under the law, the basis for who I am is in me and what I can or can't do, not in Christ and what he has done. Interestingly, it is possible to think performance matters, even that it is highly important, without basing our identity on it.

DIFFERENCES BETWEEN THE LAW AND GRACE PERSPECTIVES

Let's explore the sometimes subtle differences between the "under law" perspective and the "under grace" perspective using a series of comparison charts.

View of the law

UNDER LAW	UNDER GRACE
A set of detailed obligations that I must keep	The underlying principles of the law describe the ultimate goal toward which God is moving me:
Rigid application of case law	a loving life-style

As we saw earlier, believers under grace view the law differently than those under law. Under grace we are interested in the ethical principles of the law—the big picture. Under law, the big picture is exactly what we don't want to see. It reminds us too much of our failing performance.

Let's think again about "straining out the gnat." Why was Jesus upset about this practice? Jesus wasn't saying that it was immoral to tithe one's mint, dill, and cumin as the Pharisees were doing. But how odd that they would ever think of such a thing in the first place! How could people who are wrestling with the real moral issues of the law—absolute devotion to God, love of others, and dealing with selfishness—find the time to worry about tithing their spice box?

The answer is that they don't do both. Jesus said they "neglected the weightier provisions of the law: justice and mercy and faithfulness" (Matthew 23:23). The Pharisees' so focused on legalistic compliance with details of the law that they missed the big picture. Jesus implied that this missing of the big picture was intentional—"swallowing the camel."

At a group I used to teach we reached a young man who had grown up in a legalistic church. When we found him he was away from God, living in immorality. But he decided to return to God like a prodigal son to his father. However, his legalistic attitudes were deeply ingrained. He found it hard to resist the urge to judge others for minor infractions of the law and would regularly point out people's sins to them and to others.

The strange part was that, at the same time he judged others for minor faults like saying an off-color word, he continued to periodically engage in serious sexual immorality. I began to notice how he would become agitated about someone in the group smoking or listening to music with dirty lyrics, only to admit days later (or have his partner admit), that he had again fallen into sexual sin. It eventually got to the point where whenever he started pointing the finger or giving little sermonettes about the evils of going to bars or cussing, I would look for a chance to ask, "Have you fallen into sexual sin again?" He almost always had.

This is not an isolated pattern, as anyone who tries to work with recovering legalists knows. Being engrossed with trivial sins (or even with actions that aren't really sinful) is a sign that someone is avoiding an honest look at "the weightier portions of the law," and the proof is that major serious sin is right there in the person's life. This failure to value the things God says are important—and the corresponding tendency to harp on things that receive little emphasis in the Bible—is a symptom of legalism. The trivial issues are the matador's cape, neatly guiding attention away from the real issues. People under grace feel no need to create this distraction from the important to the trivial.

In legalistic systems, it is possible for members to feel they are doing well because they avoid certain areas of sin and they have their daily quiet time. But the real truth may be that they aren't living for God at all, and could hardly be more selfish. Legalistic systems find it necessary to create superficial definitions of sin. They usually downplay sins of omission like failure to love others, or invisible sins like living for career and money. They focus on the external more than the internal. Yet the strange strictness when it comes to certain select sins should be a clue that they are hiding something.

When Adam and Eve appeared before God in some sort of fig-leaf clothing, they wanted to talk about a pseudo-issue—that they needed to deal with their nakedness. But before they could go far discussing their version of the problem, God cut to the heart of the issue, asking, "Have you eaten of the tree from the tree of which I commanded you not to eat?" (Genesis 3:11).

Do you see what was happening when Adam and Eve diverted attention to their nakedness when they had just failed in the very heart of what God wanted them to do? God knew their fig leaves were a pointless effort to mask their sense of shame and guilt over their disobedience. Unfortunately, the human race has not left off sewing fig leaves, and now we often use the Law of God as our leaves.

View of self

UNDER LAW	UNDER GRACE
I am regenerate, and therefore I am able to keep the law.	I am regenerate, but I still can't keep the law, because of my "outer man."
The law helps my growth with God.	By relying on the Spirit, not the letter, I can gradually change. The law is not helpful here.

One of the easiest ways to discern whether people are under law is to find out how they view the law in relation to spiritual growth. Do they advocate focusing on the law for spiritual growth, or do they think focusing on the law is a hindrance to spiritual growth?

Some authors and teachers claim that we can simply face the law and comply now that we are converted. But Paul clearly draws a distinction between being under law and walking by the Spirit. For instance, in Galatians 5:18 he says, "If you are led by the Spirit, you are not under law." This is an either-or proposition. We can not have both at once. Notice also that in the context of this statement to the Galatians, both alternatives—of being under law and of following the Spirit—apply to Christians, not to non-Christians.

Also here in Romans 7:14-24, Paul describes the failure and despair of a man who is focused on the law and on "that which I am doing." The whole description teaches that focusing on self, the law, and one's works is a path leading to defeat.

Some Christian teachers no doubt do teach an overly permissive view that discounts the importance of sin. This is common in groups were the theology is more liberal. I am not arguing for a loose view of sin. I am arguing in favor of grace, and that's totally different. The Christian under grace looks to the power of the Holy Spirit, not the law, for help in living for God. The question is not whether God wants us to live a righteous life but how we get there.

Looseness is not the cure for legalism any more than legalism is the cure for looseness. Both of these false views are bad and cannot heal each other. Only a rejection of both and a decisive acceptance of God's position holds any hope.

View of the Holy Spirit

UNDER LAW	UNDER GRACE
Little practical understanding of the Spirit's ministries	Depends on the Holy Spirit for all power, motivation, and direction

No law-oriented teacher would say that the Holy Spirit is unnecessary. But their discussion of the Holy Spirit's role in spiritual growth is often vague and unclear. Sometimes we get the feeling that the Spirit is being stuck on at the end, like tipping one's hat, rather than occupying the center of the discussion. In particular, they find it very difficult to explain what Paul means when he says that we now serve "in newness of the Spirit and not in oldness of the letter" (Romans 7:6).

When I studied systematic theology in seminary, we used a thick mainstream evangelical theology text. Our teacher pointed out with dismay how odd it was to find that this volume of seven hundred pages devoted less than two pages to the ministries of the Holy Spirit! The ministries of the Spirit seem to be receiving more attention today, but many teachers still have not grasped that walking according to the Spirit and a focus on law are mutually exclusive.

The "key" to spiritual growth

UNDER LAW	UNDER GRACE
Self discipline or Special experiences	Knows self-effort is futile Romans 7:18 Looks to a process, not to quick-fix experiences

Sometimes people like to point out that one of the fruits of the Spirit is self-control (Galatians 5:23). They may overlook the fact that self-control is the *result* of walking by the Spirit, not the means to that end. In some teachers' minds it seems like Galatians 5:16 must read, "Do not fulfill the desire of the flesh and you will walk by the Spirit." But the verse actually reads, "Walk by the Spirit, and you will not fulfill the desires of the flesh." This is not a minor distinction. It's the difference between cause and effect, between law and grace. Does the power for change come from me, or does it come from God?

The same goes for many passages in the New Testament that extol various aspects of righteous living. These passages are all imperatives that depend on the indicatives; they call for our response to what God has done. For instance, James says, "Faith without works is dead" (James 2:26). Authentic faith will issue in good works because the Spirit will transform the one who walks in faith. But it would be foolish to think that doing good works is walking in faith. We will see in the next chapter how walking according to the Spirit issues in good works via grace, not law.

The tree of self-effort is barren, especially to the honest Christian. Usually, Christians under law eventually sense this barrenness. As they search for relief from chronic failure, their hearts sense a vacuum within. Into this vacuum comes the promise of a special experience, an anointing, a healing, or secret knowledge that will make everything all right. Just as some economically disadvantaged people are vulnerable to "get-rich-quick" schemes, the defeated, law-living Christian is highly vulnerable to short-cut plans that yield instant spiritual maturity or escape from personal problems.

Today's Christian culture touts various experiences that can provide healing in a short time. Many of these experiences are perfectly legitimate in the right context. The problem comes when we view them as the cure-all or shortcut for fixing our fallen natures. Some may come to view a new form of worship experience as the cure-all. Others conclude that finally realizing how badly they have been victimized will set them free from their problems. Still others determine that they need to have some people lay their hands on them and cast out the devils of selfishness or depression.

Unfortunately, none of these will provide a shortcut to anything, even though some could be helpful in certain cases. We may experience some freedom from shame by exploring our victimization, but this is no missing key to instant growth. When defeated Christians living under law conclude that these experiences are the key, they become a new legalism—yet another claim that this is how we can keep the law.

We need to accept this once and for all: There are no shortcuts to spiritual maturity. There are no quick fixes for our fallen nature.

Approach to Jesus' teaching

UNDER LAW	UNDER GRACE
Relies on inconsistent interpretation and is unable to harmonize Jesus and the epistles	Is consistent, and is able to harmonize the gospels and epistles

Modern legalistic interpreters often rely on the words of Jesus in certain sections of the Gospels to establish their law thesis.

Jesus was indeed a teacher of the law. Galatians 4:4 affirms that Jesus was "born of a woman, born under the Law." He spoke in a milieu where people actually thought they were keeping the law. His first mission was to clarify the true meaning of the law so people would understand how far short they were falling. Only then could his legalistic audience accept their need for grace. This pattern—where we must first look intently into the full demand of the law before we can fully turn to grace—is common in the New Testament, including the book of Romans, where Paul takes the same approach.

So, Jesus had to preach the law—and not the superficial version the Pharisees were using. In discourses like the Sermon on the Mount, Jesus powerfully declared the true intention of the law: perfection in thought, word, and deed. He even comes right out and says, "Therefore you are to be perfect, as your heavenly Father is perfect" (Matthew 5:48). At other times, Jesus taught grace, like with the woman at the well in John 4. He ministered in a unique period situated between the Old and New Covenants.

When modern interpreters take Jesus' law teachings and try to make them the center post of a legalistic theology, they completely miss Jesus' point. Naturally, they also run into inconsistencies with real life as well as contradictions with the rest of the New Testament. But these interpreters simply ignore or gloss over such contradictions. They also disregard the principle that the correct interpretation is the one that explains all the material in the Bible, not just one passage at the expense of another. God has given us his word, and the best way to avoid distorting it is to interpret the Bible in light of itself. God's program may change during different periods of history, but he will not contradict himself.

Some law-oriented interpreters actually revel in the contradictions generated by their system of thought. One recent author comes right out and says, "The fact is, salvation is absolutely free, but salvation will cost you everything." This statement is not just a seeming paradox; it's outright nonsense. Suppose everything you have is one million value units. According to this statement, one million equals zero. If we feel no need to make sense in our interpretations, then interpretation itself becomes a complete waste of time. We might as well agree with the non-Christian world when it proclaims that, "You can make it say whatever you want." For that matter, we might as well forget about the Bible altogether, because we would have no way of knowing what it means.

Probably the best example of Jesus' teaching on law is the Sermon on the Mount. Volumes have been written arguing that our duty is to follow this sermon to the letter. In the Sermon on the Mount Jesus says:

> But I say to you, that everyone who looks on a woman to lust for her has committed adultery with her already in his heart. And if your right eye makes you stumble, tear it out, and throw it from

you; for it is better for you that one of the parts of your body
perish, than for your whole body to be thrown into hell.
(Matthew 5:28-29)

This is fine ethical teaching. It is wrong to desire adultery, and such a sin
would be bad enough to send one to hell. No wonder Jesus says we should
pluck out our eyes if they are causing us to lust.

How many times, according to the New Testament, would we have to be
guilty of lust before we God would sentence us to hell? The answer is crystal
clear: Even one violation of the law guarantees that we fall short of the
righteous standards of God (Galatians 3:10; James 2:10). Here the modern
legalist says "Well, if we do lust, we need to be sure to ask for forgiveness."
But that's not what Jesus says, is it? He says we should pluck out our eyes!

If we are under law for salvation, it's too late to ask for forgiveness once
we have sinned. If we could be forgiven, we would be under grace. But Jesus'
sermon reflects law, not grace. He knew that we have to face the full demands
of the law before we can appreciate grace. He was trying to convince his
self-righteous audience that they needed the grace of God because they
were sinners before the law.

When thinking about the legalistic tone of the Sermon on the Mount,
don't miss the fact that Jesus is not just teaching on the subject of spiritual
growth, but on God's terms for salvation. When he warns against lust and
bitterness, the consequence of failure is hell (Matthew 5:22, 29). So, arguing
that this sermon is simply to be followed as it is, implies nothing less than
salvation by works.

Jesus also supplied the answer to our quandary: "Do not think that I came
to abolish the Law or the Prophets; I did not come to abolish, but to fulfill"
(Matthew 5:17). Jesus is our fulfillment of the law.[1] This is the only conclusion that avoids bringing the law down to a level where we can keep it. Isn't
it ironic that Jesus' legalistic audience was guilty of bringing the law down to

---

1. The Jews of Jesus' day used the term the law and the prophets to refer to the
entire Old Testament. When Jesus says he came to fulfill the Old Testament, his
fulfillment was multifaceted. He fulfilled the predictions made about Messiah and he
fulfilled the trajectory of the Old Testament by completing all the pictures of substitu-
tion and atonement found in Old Testament temple worship. He also fulfills the
demands of the Old Testament law for absolute righteousness.

a level where they could keep it, and now modern interpreters do the same thing? Notice how the NASB translates Jesus' warning in Matthew 5:22:

> "But I tell you that anyone who is angry with his brother <u>will be subject to</u> judgment. Again, anyone who says to his brother, 'Raca,' <u>is answerable to</u> the Sanhedrin. But anyone who says, 'You fool!' <u>will be in danger of</u> the fire of hell."

All the underlined expressions are the same word in Greek. Do you see what I see? Why translate henoxos differently the third time Jesus uses it? The word means "subject to" or "liable to." Isn't it obvious that the translators weren't comfortable with Jesus' message? Commenting on this section, Alexander Bruce says, "In these words of Jesus, there is an aspect of exaggeration."[2] Bruce's view mirrors many interpreters who simply refuse to accept the radical demands of the law. To admit the full requirements of the law, one would have to also admit it cannot be kept—which is exactly what Jesus wanted his listeners (and us) to see!

By recognizing why Jesus spoke of the program of law, we discover that his program is identical to that of the rest of the New Testament. He sought to convince legalists of the hopelessness of coming to God by works. Even his own teachings, which often reflected pure grace apart from works (see, e.g. John 3:16; 4:10; 5:24; 6:29), come into focus when we admit this distinction. Living in the midst of a legalistic milieu, Jesus had to spend considerable time redefining the law for those who mistakenly believed they were already keeping it. Repeatedly, would-be followers like the rich young ruler assured Jesus that they had kept the whole law from their youth, only to have him unveil that they weren't even keeping the first law on the list (Mark 10:17-22).

We can understand the strategy of Jesus' statements as well as those of the epistles only if we interpret them in light of the unfolding plan of total grace. Jesus came to bring freedom. His burden is easy, and his yoke is light. But to enter his freedom, prideful ego must surrender, and we must admit helplessness before God's awesome law. And this is not just true for justification; it is also true for spiritual growth.

---

2. Alexander Bruce in *The Expositor's Greek Testament* on Matthew 5.

Mental focus

UNDER LAW	UNDER GRACE
My duty—doing what the rules require	Identification with Christ
	Personal relationship with God
Avoiding sin	
	Loving others as a means of growth

Suppose I have my wife write down some things she would like me to do from time to time. Then, any time she wants me to do something I pull out that list. "Sorry, it's not on the list," I inform her, and head out to do something else. This would be an odd relationship, wouldn't it? Or let's suppose I begin posting rules in different rooms of the house. Whenever my wife is in the kitchen, she has to follow the kitchen rules. When she is in the bathroom, there are the bathroom rules, and so on. Why does this type of relating seem so strange?

Surely it's because such a relationship would be rather impersonal. As persons in relationship, we usually have no need for lists of rules. We are able to respond to the wishes of the other (when we want to) based on our knowledge of what pleases the other. During those times we don't want to respond, a list of rules won't help. If we interacted via a list of rules, our focus would be on the rules, not on each other. Even in cases where a couple actually resorts to using rules while sorting out their relationship, they don't view following the rules as the final goal.

In the same way, we also need to avoid viewing the Bible as a source book for things we don't have to do. The one who comes to the Bible with this agenda has missed the point badly. God gave us the Bible to help us serve him, not to "get out of" doing his will. It is because we want to live for God that we need to come out from under the law. Our next chapter begins to explore the right way to see God's will manifested in our lives.

Reaction to failure

UNDER LAW	UNDER GRACE
Surprised and distressed	Not surprised
Rationalizations, minimization, blame-shifting and self-recrimination	Confident of God's acceptance
	Return to active dependence
Vows to do better	

God wants our focus to be on him, not on a list of rules. William Newell said, "To be disappointed in yourself is to have trusted yourself." I can't find a flaw in that reasoning. The implication is clear: When we are deeply disappointed in our performance, we have lapsed into a performance mentality. Such disappointment leads to various dishonest and sleazy tricks designed to help us live with ourselves.

The law-living Christian has great difficulty simply admitting sin. To do so without qualification threatens his identity in a way he cannot live with. The only solution is to receive our identity from Christ and give up on the whole work-righteous identity building project.

We have already mentioned the peril of making new vows to do better. We routinely break these vows, which produces even more alienation from God.

Reaction to success

UNDER LAW	UNDER GRACE
Proud and intolerant of others	Humbly grateful
	Still able to empathize with those who fail
	Sees continued need for growth

Legalists often develop a disagreeable demeanor of self-righteousness. We are all familiar with this distasteful "holier-than-thou" attitude, and none of us can honestly claim we have never had it ourselves. No wonder God wants to wean us from a focus on the law. If we harbor delusions that we are able to do good in ourselves, we will never give the glory to him. Our friends will pay a nasty price for our pride. Also, as long as we harbor these delusions, we will not come to the throne of grace with empty hands to receive God's healing.

Eventual result

UNDER LAW	UNDER GRACE
External conformity, but increasing internal defeat and hypocrisy	Gradual transformation into a person with a measure of victory over sin and a spiritual mind-set
Growing cynicism and despair *or* self-righteous external comparisons	A more loving person Transparency
Self deception	

Legalism will kill your spiritual growth and poison your relationship with God. And since we should want to see our characters change and become more Christ-like, we now turn to God's alternative: walking according to the Spirit.

PART 2: GRACE IN ACTION

THE CORRECT REACTION TO THE LAW: DEPENDENCE

U p to this point, we have been studying the theory behind our new identity in Christ. Most of these truths have been somewhat abstract. Now we follow Paul's discussion into Romans 8, where he teaches us how to apply these truths to daily life.

THE FAITH-REST WALK

We have seen that Christians failing before the Law of God react in one of three ways. We already discussed the two negative options: 1) despair, leading to apathy or even giving up, or 2) denial, leading to Phariseeism.

Now we come to the third reaction, what some have called the "faith-rest walk" with Jesus. When walking according to the Spirit we will see the power of the Holy Spirit working through us as we relate to God and others with real love. We can become free from self-absorption like never before. In its place will be the knowledge of our real significance and purpose—not just pie-in-the-sky some day, but a truly attainable walk with God where we are able to "rest" confidently in the security of Christ's love.

When we leave off trying to establish our identity through our good works, we can finally relax, and through faith, come to understand what Paul means when he says "It is no longer I who live, but Christ lives in me; and the life which I now live in the flesh I live by faith in the Son of God."

WALKING ACCORDING TO THE SPIRIT: THE BASIS, THE MEANS, AND THE GOAL

Paul repeatedly refers to "walking according to the Spirit" in Romans 8. He introduces the subject in verses 1-4:

> There is therefore now no condemnation for those who are in Christ Jesus. For the law of the Spirit of life in Christ Jesus has set you free from the law of sin and of death. For what the Law could not do, weak as it was through the flesh, God did: sending His own Son in the likeness of sinful flesh and as an offering for sin, He condemned sin in the flesh, in order that the requirement of the Law might be fulfilled in us, who do not walk according to the flesh, but according to the Spirit.

Notice several things about this passage.

Our Basis: Security

To walk in the Spirit, we need to know up front that we are secure. We will sometimes fail, but God wants us to know "there is no condemnation for those of us who are in Christ" (vs. 1). Suppose my wife asked me if I would change in some way. Probably, out of love, I would be inclined to try to accommodate her request as long as it wasn't inappropriate.

But suppose that as she asks me, she lays a .45-caliber semiautomatic on the table. I'm sure it would put a real chill on the conversation! I would probably stop talking about her request and say, "Wait a minute. What's that for?"

"Well, this is in case you won't do what I ask," she answers.

What's wrong with this picture?

This illustration highlights the importance of moving toward God in the unshakable knowledge of our unconditional acceptance in him. God lays no .45 on the table when he asks us to respond to his love.1 He wants us to come to him and follow him out of love, not fear. This is why John says, "There is no fear in love; but perfect love casts out fear, because fear involves punishment, and the one who fears is not perfected in love" (1 John 4:18). Fear is associated with legalism, not with grace. Unless we are confident in God's view of us, we will not have "bold access" to him, as the author of Hebrews calls it (Hebrews 4:16). Resting in Christ requires that we know we are secure.

Our Means: The Finished Work of Christ

The next step is to realize God has already done it all. In verses 2 and 3 of Romans 8 Paul says, "For the law of the Spirit of life in Christ Jesus has set you free from the law of sin and of death. For what the Law could not do, weak as it was through the flesh, God did." This is a restatement of what we have called "the indicative." That is, God always starts with what he has already done and then moves to our response to that truth. The pattern of grace is, "Because God has acted, I want to respond." The pattern for law is the opposite: "*If* I act, God will respond." Who is the doer, and who is the

---

1. We should be aware that the King James Version has a different reading for verse 1. That version says, "There is therefore no condemnation for them which are in Christ Jesus, *who walk not after the flesh but after the Spirit*" (emphasis added). You can see that the last phrase puts a condition on the promise, giving it a completely different meaning. If this reading were correct, our acceptance would depend on our ability to walk after the Spirit. Apparently, the promise doesn't apply if we walk after the flesh. However, this reading is mistaken.

The last phrase belongs in verse 4 and was incorrectly copied onto the end of verse 1. None of the earliest and best manuscripts have this reading. However, the most ancient manuscripts were not available at the time the King James Version was written. Fortunately, we see remarkably few errors of this kind in the New Testament.

Of course, those of us who believe that the Bible is inspired and without error when originally written know that there are some copyist errors in every manuscript we have. This doesn't affect the reliability of the Bible, because by comparing the thousands of ancient manuscripts in our possession, we can determine with a high degree of accuracy what the originals said. Besides, the errors in copying hardly ever affect the meaning of the text in any significant way. However, this particular error in the King James Version powerfully affects a key doctrine, distorting the meaning of this important unconditional promise. The New King James Version has correctly noted that this reading is an error. The truth is, there is no condemnation for those who are in Christ Jesus.

responder? This is the first and biggest question, and one that we have already dealt with adequately.

OUR GOAL: CHRIST-LIKE CHARACTER

Paul reveals that God's work was done "in order that the requirement of the Law might be fulfilled in us, who do not walk according to the flesh, but according to the Spirit." This verse promises that the requirements of the law—goodness, or righteous character—will be evident in the lives of those who learn to walk according to the Spirit. As we saw earlier, walking Christians will end up doing the very things the Law calls for, but we arrive there via a different, or indirect, path. This is an important distinction. It is neither double talk nor a subtle reversal of what has gone before, but rather an acknowledgement that self cannot change self.

WALKING ACCORDING TO THE SPIRIT OR THE FLESH: DEFINITION

In the following verses, Paul repeatedly defines for us what he means by walking according to the Spirit:

> For those who are according to the flesh *set their minds* on the things of the flesh, but those who are according to the Spirit, [*set their minds on*] the things of the Spirit. For the *mind set on* the flesh is death, but the *mind set on* the Spirit is life and peace, because the *mind set on* the flesh is hostile toward God; for it does not subject itself to the law of God, for it is not even able to do so. (Romans 8:5-7, emphasis added)

Over and over, Paul stresses that walking according to the flesh or the Spirit is a matter of our mindset. Our struggle begins not in our behaviors, but in our thought life. The mind is the true battleground when it comes to spiritual things. What does it mean, in practical terms, to set our mind on the things of the flesh?

THE MIND SET ON THE FLESH

Before studying what it means to set our minds on the Spirit, we need to carefully consider what Paul means by setting our minds on the flesh. We may find that this fleshly mindset includes some things we never considered problematic. Many Christians mistakenly define some fleshly areas of mental focus as "good."

We have already seen one example of this—focusing on the law. Though some Christians believe that God wants them to focus on rules, Paul clearly dismisses that view in Romans 7. Now we realize that focusing on the law is the worst thing we can do.[2] Consider other aspects of mindset in Paul's description of his struggle with defeat in chapter 7:14-24. Three things stick out as primary in Paul's mind:

"I" or "me"
"That which I am doing"
"That which the Law says"

His orientation is toward himself and his performance before the Law of God. Now let's compare these to his list of things we died to in Christ, culled from Romans 6 and 7.

---

2. People wonder why David would so extol meditating on the law in Psalms 119 and parallels. The biggest problem here is really one of translation. The Hebrews used the word *torah* for law, but also for "teaching" or "instruction." The same is true for other key Hebrew words used for "statutes" "precepts" "judgments" "promises" and "decrees" in this key psalm. This psalm is a poem of love for God's word. To see how translations of these words vary, compare NIV, NASB, and NLT versions verse by verse.

PAUL'S MENTAL FOCUS IN ROMANS 7	THINGS TO WHICH WE HAVE DIED
"I" or "me"	We died to our old selves (Romans 6:6)
"That which I am doing"	We died to sin (Romans 6:11)
"That which the Law says."	We died to the Law (Romans 7:6)

The two lists match each other exactly, and this is not a coincidence. Walking according to the flesh means we set our minds on those things to which we died in Christ. This means Paul is describing walking according to the flesh in Romans 7. When God says we have died to our old self, to sin or to the law, and we nevertheless set our minds on these things, we are focusing on our old identity—our identity in Adam. In other words, we are setting our minds on the things of the flesh.

In addition to the three things detailed in Romans 7, we could add another thing to which Paul says we have died in Galatians 6:14: "But may it never be that I should boast, except in the cross of our Lord Jesus Christ, through which the world has been crucified to me, and I to the world." So, setting our minds on the "world" (Greek *kosmos*) is yet one more mindset that constitutes walking according to the flesh. Let's briefly consider each of these possible fleshly focuses before considering the alternative mindset—focusing on the things of the Spirit.

WALKING ACCORDING TO THE FLESH: SELF-FOCUS

What does it mean to set my mind on myself? Obviously, we can't help but think of ourselves. But *how* we view ourselves is critical. Are we focusing on ourselves as we were in Adam, or on ourselves as we are in Christ? In the chart below, you see how that which is true of us in Adam could characterize our thinking even as believers. But the column on the right is how we should view ourselves.

OLD SELF (IN ADAM)	NEW SELF (IN CHRIST)
ALIENATED FROM GOD Therefore, we think of our old self on a horizontal plane—me vs. my problems, others, circumstances, etc.	**ALIVE TO GOD** Therefore, we think of ourselves on both a horizontal and a vertical plane. Our interactions with others, our problems, circumstances, etc. are all considered in the light of how God is (or may be) working through them.

DOOMED TO DEATH
Therefore, everything is temporary, and temporary things are valuable. We spend our time trying to acquire or hold onto temporary things like material wealth.

GUARANTEED ETERNAL LIFE
Therefore, temporary things become only means to an end. Only things that are eternal have ultimate value (like God, the truth, and people). Our stewardship of material and natural things in this life is important mainly because these will affect our future life with God.

ALONE WITH UNMET NEEDS
Therefore, we look to others to meet the hunger of loneliness by loving us the right way. Much of our thought lives are spent trying to understand why others won't meet our needs, or how to make them meet our needs. In our pain, we pity ourselves and are often angry at God and others.

IN UNION WITH CHRIST AND WITH OTHER CHRISTIANS, OUR NEEDS MET FULLY IN CHRIST
(Romans 12:5; Ephesians 1:3)
Therefore, our focus is on how we can meet the needs of others. Instead of pitying ourselves, we find ourselves praising God for his provision.

UNCLEAR SENSE OF IDENTITY
(like the man in the bubble)
Therefore, we doubt our own acceptability and spend time seeking acceptance and affirmation from other people who assure us we are important. We spend much of our thought lives fretting about what others think of us.

IDENTITY BASED ON GOD'S VIEW OF US
Therefore, we become less concerned about what others think of us. We are able to leave the question of who we are behind as a settled matter and direct our thoughts outward, increasingly free from self-doubt and man-pleasing.

GUILTY OF SIN	FORGIVEN COMPLETELY, DEAD TO SIN
We *feel* guilty because we *are* guilty. When our mind is set on the old self, we experience an abiding sense of shame that depresses us and robs us of motivation. Our focus locks increasingly onto self, bringing distance into all our relationships.	We are able to look away from sin, laying it aside at the cross of Christ. Our thought life is spent contemplating how we may accomplish spiritual goals, not on how we failed earlier.

In biblical terms, people who are selfish, or self-centered, are people who see themselves in their old identity in Adam. The resulting problems cause more intense self-absorption, anxiety, and efforts to manipulate situations and people. Negative self-centeredness is an effort to establish our own identity through temporal, finite means. People, money, glory, and temporal security are all at-risk bases for identity. The state of affairs in these areas could change at any moment.

When we see ourselves in Christ only, we are practicing in a sense, a Christ-centered focus, even when we are thinking of ourselves. This is clear from passages like Colossians 3:1-3:

> If then you have been raised up with Christ, keep seeking the things above, where Christ is, seated at the right hand of God. Set your mind on the things above, not on the things that are on earth. For you have died and your life is hidden with Christ in God.

This call to "set our minds" on the things above is based on the fact that this is where our new identity lies. This is how we can think of ourselves without being self-absorbed in the negative sense.

THE VANISHING RETURNS OF SELF-ABSORPTION

We saw earlier that the more we focus on our sin problems, the worse they become. Although it is counter-intuitive, the same is true when we focus on self. The more we focus on what we don't have and how we can meet our own needs, the more intense our dissatisfaction becomes. The more we focus on how to get others to meet our needs, the more unacceptable their attempts to do so become.

Self-focused people live out the truth of Jesus' riddle: "Whoever wishes to save his life will lose it, but whoever loses his life for my sake, he is the one who will save it" (Luke 9:24.)

As their lives progress, they may become more and more demanding and more and more disappointed in people. Some turn to anger, others to sorrow and withdrawal, but the cause is the same. As we walk according to the flesh, we are looking to ourselves, our circumstances, and others for something they can never supply. Only God can meet our personal needs for significance, identity, and love.

Why not turn to God at this moment and offer to begin viewing yourself as you are in Christ, instead of in Adam?

PROBLEMS WITH MODERN THEORIES

We know from Romans 7 that self-focus is walking according to the flesh. But this view flatly contradicts much of what many today (including many Christians) believe. People today think focusing on themselves is the key to happiness and health. Modern people believe they will solve their problems by "centering themselves," "being true to themselves," or "gaining a sense of self." Embracing the pain of past abuse and mourning over it will also help us heal, they argue.

Christian thinkers are confused about these therapeutic suggestions. On one side is the observation that some people, especially victims of abuse as children, seem to forget sections of their early lives or idealize a past that was horrible. This is usually a sign of repression or denial—defense mechanisms that can threaten people's ability to stay in touch with reality and to relate to others honestly.

On the other side is the self-obsession that doesn't heal and only creates more fury and ingratitude in life. I know counseling clients who have been peeling back layers of victimization for over a decade now and are just as mean, reproachful, and self-absorbed as ever. While certain people may need to focus on themselves and their past episodes of abuse for a period of time, this should not be the norm.

GETTING OUTSIDE YOURSELF

God wants to liberate us from a self-centered focus and help us develop a Christ-centered focus. Learning to cultivate gratitude for what God has given us in Christ (which we did not deserve) is more therapeutic than ruminating endlessly over past hurts. "The mind set on the Spirit is life and peace" (Romans 8:6).

Jesus also taught that loving God and loving others are the central elements in Christian living. That means we need to learn to focus on others' needs, which isn't possible while we're self-absorbed. Developing an others-centered perspective is an effective counter to self absorption.

WALKING ACCORDING TO THE FLESH: SIN FOCUS

Christians have died to sin (Romans 6:10). Therefore, setting our minds on sin amounts to setting our minds on the things of the flesh. Many Christians find their times of prayer breaking down mainly because they feel such shame before God that communication with him is difficult. The accuser of the brethren is also constantly fanning the flames of guilt and shame, because he knows how quickly these break down our relationship with God.

CONFESSION

Yet many devotional teachers argue that the first thing we should do when getting together with the Lord is think of every sin we committed since the last time we were with him. They argue that after identifying sins we have committed, we can confess them and receive cleansing. This, they argue, allows us to put our sin behind us.

The Scriptural basis for this approach to God is thin, mainly relying on 1 John 1:9 which says, "If we confess our sins, He is faithful and righteous to forgive us our sins and to cleanse us from all unrighteousness." This verse has gained an inordinate importance in some groups, to the point where they end up quoting it every week. But important truths are normally repeated in many passages. This raises doubts about whether some modern teaching on this practice is biblically balanced.

In the first place, this passage in 1 John is not speaking to the issue of devotional time with God. Rather the context is a comparison between orthodox Christian theology and a heretical, dualistic ideology. Dualists in John's day denied that they were sinful, because they held that bodily action doesn't count as sin. So instead of admitting they were sinners, like true Christians do, they were denying their sin (vs. 8, 10).

John compares and contrasts these two views repeatedly in this section. By comparing the parallel construction in verses 6, 8, and 10 on one hand, and verses 7 and 9 on the other, we see that John is comparing Christians and heretics, not walking and fleshly Christians. Notice that the implied penalty for not confessing our sinfulness is that we are *neither forgiven nor cleansed of sin* (v. 9). How could such a conditional statement be a prescription for Christians' devotional time with God?

When sins weigh heavily on our minds, we should confess and resolve them before God. The importance of confession is that from *our* side we are feeling shame over our wrongdoing. Confession means agreeing with God. In other words, we admit that what we did was wrong, and that it was our fault, not someone else's. We can then appropriate God's grace anew. Psalms 32 and 51, along with parallel passages, teach on the need to resolve unconfessed sin with God. However, to suggest that this is how we should begin every time with God is not biblically warranted.

ASKING FORGIVENESS

Many devotional teachers also suggest asking God for forgiveness when you confess sin. But this practice is also unwarranted. Instead of asking God to forgive us, we should thank him for having already forgiven us. The idea of asking for and obtaining forgiveness as you go in life is an Old Covenant teaching. We never see this in New Testament teaching after Pentecost. That's because we don't receive forgiveness one bit at a time; we receive it once and for all (Hebrews 10:12, 14).

Remember, even Jesus' prayer, "Forgive us our transgressions," was from the Old Covenant period. Compare his statement, "If you do not forgive others, then your Father will not forgive your transgressions" (Matthew 6:14-15), with Paul's statement after Pentecost in Ephesians 4:32 "Be kind to one another, tender-hearted, forgiving each other, just as God in Christ also has forgiven you." Notice the verb tense for "has forgiven." It's the tense of already completed action, whereas Jesus' statement is conditional: God will forgive you only if you forgive.

The doctrine of confession, absolution, and forgiveness goes far back into church history, and is more linked to the Old Testament sacrificial system than to New Covenant teaching. The fixation on detailed confession was also linked to the re-introduction of priests and a "pay as you go" interpretation of the Lord's Supper, according to which the mass procures forgiveness for the sins you committed that week. It has no place in biblical Christianity.

THE IMPACT OF FOCUSING ON SIN

Christians who focus on this daily cleansing easily develop a sin focus in their prayer lives. Every time they come to God in prayer, sin is on their minds. Often, the whole time is spent in hand-wringing regret over sin. This is not walking according to the Spirit. Rather, it matches exactly Paul's description of a defeated believer in Romans 7.

Believers may even come to believe that God has laid the .45-caliber semiautomatic on the table—the real threat of rejection by God. This would have a chilling effect on anyone's relationship with God.

God is willing to take the risk of granting us full once-for-all forgiveness. For those interested, the following chart summarizes some of the important passages on the subject.

These verses and many others teach that our salvation is secure and our forgiveness is once-for-all at the time we receive the gift of salvation.

EPHESIANS 2:8-9	Salvation is "by grace …through faith. It is not the result of works." If our forgiveness has to be gained by our confession and daily request, it is contingent on works we do. These verses will not allow that.
EPHESIANS 4:32	God in Christ "has forgiven" us. The tense of the verb here means forgiveness is a completed action.

COLOSSIANS 2:13	"When you were dead in your transgressions… He made you alive together with Him, having forgiven us all our transgressions." If all our transgressions have been forgiven, why do we need to continue to ask for forgiveness?
ROMANS 8:1	"There is no condemnation for those in Christ Jesus."
JOHN 5:24	If anyone believes in Christ, he "does not come into judgment, but passes out of death and into life."
HEBREWS 10:14	God "has perfected for all time those who are set apart."
EPHESIANS 1:13-14	God has "sealed" us in Christ with the Holy Spirit. This verse alludes to a wax seal placed on scrolls so they could not be opened before they were delivered to the recipient. It means we will not be lost before our entrance to heaven.
ROMANS. 8:29; EPHESIANS 1:4-5	The term "predestined" means to set or fix someone's ultimate destiny. God has set the believer's ultimate destiny. We will be conformed to Christ, or made holy and blameless, at Christ's return (cf. Philippians 3:21).

THE RESULT OF TOTAL GRACE

Will people who know they are secure with God become soft on sin and take advantage of the grace of God? Perhaps. But if they do, they have not understood grace correctly. Even Paul sometimes felt it was necessary to remind believers that people are going to Hell because of sin, so it should never be viewed as unimportant.[1]

---

1. 1 Corinthians 6:9-11; Ephesians 5:5-7; Galatians 5:19-21. In each of these pas-

Sin *is* important—so much so that Jesus died to forgive it. But the sad irony is that if we develop a sin focus in our lives, we will fall ever deeper into the grip of sin, like a man struggling in quicksand. This was Paul's fate in Romans 7:14-24, before he looked away from "that which I am doing" and toward Christ. The power that sets us free from sin comes, not from dwelling on how bad it is, but by dwelling on the "things of the Spirit," including our sinless identity in Christ.

We could also focus on sin not because we feel bad about our sin, but because we are lusting for sin. When believers spend time lusting and thirsting for opportunities to commit sin, or reminiscing about favorite sin episodes of the past, they are also setting their minds on the things of the flesh. We probably don't need to say a great deal about this because it's so obvious. Clearly, the key to such situations is learning to turn our attention to something more positive: the things of the Spirit. It also helps to have well-developed relationships that become more rewarding than sin.

A CORRECTED FOCUS

We have already seen that God wants us to "present [ourselves] to him as those alive from the dead" (Romans 6:13). This means we should come to him, focusing not on our sins, but on who we are in Christ. We saw that the key to walking according to the Spirit is to set our minds on the things of

---

sages, the reasoning is the same. He is not threatening the believer with Hell. Rather, he is arguing that, since people are going to be judged and sent to Hell for such actions, they should have no place in lives of believers. Yet it's clear that in Corinth believers were actually engaging in some if not all of the behaviors he mentions, and this is why he brings it up. Paul argues that, though believers might do such things, it is totally inappropriate because "you were washed, but you were sanctified, but you were justified in the name of the Lord Jesus Christ" (1 Corinthians 6:11).

Likewise in Ephesians 5:5-8, he lists some sins and says "Let no one deceive you with empty words, for because of these things the wrath of God comes upon the sons of disobedience." Is he threatening his readers? No! He goes on to say, "Therefore do not be partakers with *them*." Again, it must be possible to partake in these deeds, or Paul would have no reason to write this passage. But while it is possible for a Christian to partake in the deeds of darkness, his identity would not become that of "a son of disobedience." On the contrary, he reminds them, "You were formerly darkness, but now you are light in the Lord; walk as children of light" (verse 8). Our identity is forever set, and therefore we should not behave like those who have another identity. The thinking here is consistent throughout the New Testament. In none of these passages is Paul threatening his readers with condemnation.

the Spirit. But sin is a thing of the flesh, not a thing of the Spirit. To set our minds on sin is to set our minds on things of the flesh.

Yes, there are times when we feel burdened by unresolved sin, and we need to confess it and thank God for our forgiveness. But this is different than having a sin *focus*. God will let us know if there is a sin issue we need to deal with. The practice of cataloguing our sins is pointless and wrongheaded.

Many of us need to change our approach to our times with God. Instead of sitting down with God and counting up all our sins, try sitting down and counting up all the things he has done for you! Review the miracle of your forgiveness and your marvelous new identity in Jesus. Thank and praise God for who you are in Christ. You may need to consciously and even verbally review the truths of your identification with Christ. Say to God, "I'm not coming to you based on any of my works, which I know are sinful, but entirely based on the grace of Christ."

This is Paul's point in Philippians 4:8, which *is* discussing our devotional prayer lives:

> Finally, brethren, whatever is true, whatever is honorable, whatever is right, whatever is pure, whatever is lovely, whatever is of good repute, if there is any excellence and if anything worthy of praise, let your mind dwell on these things.

Some Christians are virtually obsessed with their sins, and every time they look to God, the only thing they can think of is all the sins they have committed. (Of course others are so self-righteous that they hardly notice their own sin, and this is also a problem.) When we are obsessed with sin, we are seeing the sin-focus at its worst, completely disrupting our relationship with our Lord and condemning us to a miserable life of walking according to the flesh.

No wonder Satan, the accuser, is so intent on pressing our sins upon us, as though our identity had never changed. We all face an ongoing struggle as we attempt to look away from what we have done and toward what God has done for us.

WALKING ACCORDING TO THE FLESH: KOSMOS FOCUS

Paul says that through the cross of Christ "the world has been crucified to me, and I to the world" (Galatians 6:14). We argued that in Romans 8:4-8, setting our minds on the things of the flesh means setting our minds on things to which we have died in Christ, so this includes the world-system. The term "world," (*kosmos* in Greek) is a special word in the New Testament. In most uses, the *kosmos* refers not to the world in the sense of the physical globe, but to a system of values. In 1 John 2:15 God says:

> Do not love the *kosmos*, nor the things in the *kosmos*. If anyone loves the *kosmos*, the love of the Father is not in him. For all that is in the *kosmos*, the lust of the flesh and the lust of the eyes and the boastful pride of life, is not from the Father, but is from the *kosmos*.

Kosmos describes the perspective of humankind without God, as well as the system humans have developed apart from God's leadership. The world system values temporary things like money, prestige, and sensual experience more than eternal things. Therefore, it stands opposed to God's values system.

Strangely, even Christians' values systems are sometimes based on things like the boastful pride of life, the lust of the eyes, and the lust of the flesh. Modern Christians often have difficulty seeing what is wrong with valuing the *kosmos*, even though God reserves some of his strongest words to warn us not to love it. For instance, James says, "Do you not know that friendship with the *kosmos* is hostility toward God?" (James 4:4).

One reason for such strong language is the fact that the *kosmos* is really the kingdom of God's enemy, Satan. Repeatedly in the New Testament, Satan is called the ruler of this *kosmos* (John 12:31; 14:30; 16:11). In Ephesians 6:12 demons who are the "world rulers" of this darkness are the *kosmoskrators*. John says "the whole *kosmos* lies in the power of the evil one" (1 John 5:19). No wonder God is not pleased when his followers adore the system ruled by his enemy, the destroyer of human souls!

Things like money, pleasure, and career have a certain value, and we are free to enjoy them in the right context. However, each can become an idol, replacing God's place in our lives with an addiction.

Let's take money as an example. There is nothing wrong with money per se, and everyone must make and use money. Working to earn money is the will of God (Ephesians 4:28). But in the *kosmos*, people look to money as their source of happiness and identity. As a result, it takes on an importance that is out of proportion to reality. Some people are prepared to devote their lives to the acquisition of money, even to the extent that they ruin their relationships, their families, and their own physical and emotional health. Money is the idol of choice in America.

A BASEMENT FULL OF FORKS

Perhaps if we change the terminology a bit, it will be easier to understand God's point of view in this area. Instead of thinking of dollars, suppose we think of forks. A fork is made of metal, and most forks cost a certain amount of money. A set of a dozen forks has a certain value, especially if they are nice forks. They not only have resale value, but are also useful when we eat food. Therefore, I doubt any of us would argue that forks are without value. Neither would we say it's a sin to own forks. In fact, all of us probably have some forks in our homes.

But suppose a certain man became fascinated with forks and began to collect them. Every day his fork collection becomes larger and larger as he steadily acquires forks from every source. Eventually, his basement begins to fill up with forks, until he is undoubtedly the foremost fork owner in the world. He realizes that he owns millions of forks, including some very costly ones from Europe. Some of his friends occasionally chide him, arguing that there are better things to do in life than buying and collecting forks. But he just smiles. He knows they only say that because they have so few forks themselves. They're obviously jealous!

One night he comes home very late, as usual. His kids complain, "Dad, where were you? We wanted to spend some time with you."

As he drags a wood box in the door, he answers, "I found some great forks! Check out this whole crate I got."

As they groan and roll their eyes, he only replies, "You guys just don't know the value of a fork!"

We may find this story laughable, but only because forks are neither agreed upon legal tender nor a common thing to collect. But the things we do collect are no different. Whether we amass clothes, cars, real estate, sports equipment, or dollars in the bank, these could all be converted into forks in terms of their lasting value.

Jesus taught about a man who had spent his life filling seven large barns with grain—another thing most of us wouldn't want today. But in that day, grain was even better than money. It might as well have been forks, though, because when the man died he lost all of it anyway (Luke 12:16-21).

The legalistic thinker might speak up at this point and say, "I think anyone with more than eight forks in his home is wasting the Lord's money!" But this is not the point. Which of us has more forks doesn't matter. What matters is that we have a sense of proportion in our lives—something our fork collector obviously doesn't have. We can buy, own, and use forks without falling in love with them or allowing our fork mania to interfere with our relationships and our Christian ministry.

To put it differently, we shouldn't try to draw our identity from our forks.

Those who draw their identity from their forks spend all their time thinking about forks. Their minds are set on the things of the flesh. This is the real point as far as God is concerned. When people develop an unhealthy obsession with the things of the world, it becomes impossible for them to set their minds on the things of the Spirit.

FREEDOM FROM THE KOSMOS

John gives us one key to freedom when interacting with the world system. After the passage we read earlier about not loving the things of the world, he goes on to say, "And the *kosmos* is passing away, and also its lusts; but the one who does the will of God abides forever" (1 John 2:17). Here is the key to an effective critique of the values system of the world. Only that which is permanent is truly valuable, and things that are permanent are spiritual things.

What if someone offered you a million dollars to kill yourself? Not very tempting. What if they raised the offer to a hundred million? Still not tempting? It's too obvious! What good is a bunch of money if I can't enjoy it after I earn it? Suppose he offers to pay you now, and you can wait five hours to kill yourself, or even five hundred hours? I still wouldn't be tempted. How could I enjoy the money, knowing where it's all headed? This is the way our lives are if we live for the things of the *kosmos*.

WHY DOES THIS HAPPEN?

An eternal values system makes sense, especially for a Christian. But how is it that our minds continually slip back into a temporal values system?

Within each of us is a deep-seated desire to feel loved and significant. In our lostness we learn to divert this thirst to things like money, acclaim, prestige, and sensual experiences. None of these can really meet our inner needs, but like heroin to the junkie, they ease the pain for awhile. We live in an age often characterized by secular thinkers as an age of freedom. But the truth is that we live in the age of addiction. As people, including Christians, try to satisfy their inner needs through the values system of the *kosmos*, they become more and more thirsty and obsessed.

Even for Christians, fixation on the things of the world will not easily disappear. Most of us spend a substantial part of every day mentally focused on the things of the *kosmos*. And unless we consciously bring God into our thinking, all our time ill be spent walking according to the flesh.

ASSESSING HONESTLY

What's the solution? Withdrawal to a monastery where our thinking won't be invaded as often by evil? No. This is human thinking again—seeking to control the inner attitude by controlling the outer environment. Paul deplores any attempt to withdraw from evil via withdrawal from the *kosmos*. In 1 Corinthians 5:9-10 he says:

> I wrote you in my letter not to associate with immoral people;
> I did not at all mean with the immoral people of this *kosmos*, or
> with the covetous and swindlers, or with idolaters; for then you
> would have to go out of the *kosmos*.

He wanted them to avoid immoral Christians as a form of discipline. Clearly, it would be unthinkable that we should try to avoid immoral non-Christians, because this would mean going "out of the world." We would be depriving the world of the very light it needs. This is also why Jesus said, when praying for his disciples, "I do not ask you to take them out of the *kosmos*, but to keep them from the evil one" (John 17:15). Trying to escape the *kosmos* is not the answer.

OVERSEEING OUR MINDSET

Recognizing that we spend much of our time with our mind set on the things of the flesh can be depressing. But all is not lost. We need to avoid making matters worse by having the wrong reaction.

The key to progress is not to count up the minutes we spend focused on the things of the Spirit or the flesh, thus creating a new legalism. Instead, we should learn to look away from our own "score" of where we have logged the most time mentally and simply turn our focus back to Jesus.

God gives us information about the importance of our mindset so we will understand the direction we need to take, not so we can obsessively take our spiritual temperature. If we focus on our performance in this area, we become spiritual hypochondriacs. Hypochondriacs worry and fuss about their health instead of simply doing healthy things and letting God and nature do the rest. Likewise, spiritual hypochondriacs end up focused on self in a way that does no good.

God never says we have to log more hours focusing on the things of the Spirit than on the things of the flesh. The ratio between these two is never specified. Instead, when we realize we are focusing on the things of the flesh, we have the opportunity to immediately change our focus to the things of the Spirit. If we sit fretting about how little we have focused on God lately, we prolong the time spent walking in the flesh. Instead, we should quit worrying about how long or how deep our latest excursion into the flesh has been and immediately reestablish fellowship with our waiting father.

THE CUMULATIVE EFFECT

No matter how little time I spend truly focused on the things of the Spirit during a given day, that time counts. During such times I release the power of the Spirit into my thinking and my life, and he will work accordingly. If I do the same the next day, he'll work again. At the end of a year, these times with

God add up perhaps to an embarrassingly small total period spent focused on the things of the Spirit. Yet these are the times God was free to work unfettered, and the result will be tangible.

After another year the pile of times spent with God will be larger, and after five or ten years it may be substantial. I will find that God has worked during these times, often so slowly as to seem imperceptible. After ten years, the changes in my life will probably be quite perceptible, unless the whole process has consistently been short-circuited by some grace-slaying perspective I might harbor—especially legalism or rebellion.

Are we prepared to come before God at this moment and admit that we've spent entirely too much time trying to deny our fleshliness or fretting over how helpless we feel? Are we prepared to set these thoughts aside and immediately reach out to accept the hand God is offering us? Can we leave the negativity of legalistic apathy behind and again surrender to the love of God? If so, we are ready to consider what is involved in walking according to the Spirit.

WALKING ACCORDING TO THE SPIRIT: PRAYER

od provides various channels, or means, through which we can mind the things of the Spirit. The Bible teaches that God's blessing will come into our lives, not primarily in some general, mystical way, but through these channels, which could be called the means of growth.

We have argued up to this point that legalism is a deadly threat to authentic spiritual growth. This is never truer than when we consider how to set our minds on the things of the Spirit through the means of growth.

Under the legalistic paradigm, these means of growth become duties that seem to pump power up from within ourselves or that rack up brownie points, rather than ways to receive the power of God. Often this school of thought includes a menacing collection of threats for those who fail to partake of these means of growth in sufficient measure. Such threats create the fear needed for motivation in the legalistic thought system.

We need to rethink each of the means of growth, considering not only what they are, but also what they are not. For every thesis there is an antithesis, and the antithesis of God's program of growth in love is the legalistic model of tooth-gritting adherence to a code while bobbing and weaving to avoid dangerous sanctions along the way. Put differently, God's program is doing arising out of being. Legalism is when we *do* in order to *be*.[1]

PRAYER: DIRECT RELATIONSHIP

Paul teaches that the key to walking according to the Spirit is to "set our minds on the things of the Spirit." The most obvious way to do this is through prayer. Nothing is more personal or more important in our relationship with God than our prayer lives. Our times of prayer have the potential to be the most refreshing and reassuring times in our lives. This is possible only if we stay away from understanding prayer as a formalistic exercise more suited to a machine than a personal relationship.

GET A TIME

To develop a good prayer life, you need to designate a time for drawing close to God through his word and prayer. You need a focused time to put aside the day's business, stimulation, and activity. Drawing close to God takes some time. You should turn off the TV or computer screen (unless you have the discipline to use your computer Bible and journaling capabilities without yielding to the temptation to check your Facebook).

Morning is best. You don't need an hour or two to do this. It's far more important to get a regular habit than to spend tons of time. If you start with twenty to thirty minutes and get regular time (that is, every day), you can add time later. I find that some people tell themselves they don't have time because they're thinking they need an hour or more, so they just do nothing.

Start with a reading from scripture. As you do this, ask God to show you what he wants you to see. We'll discuss ideas for getting into the word in the next chapter.

When you pray, you must begin correctly. Start by reviewing your new identity like we discussed in Chapters 5 and 6. Thanksgiving is very important before getting into your requests. Spend time remembering who God is and what he has done for you. "Take your seat" in Christ.

If you take your time on this part, you may notice that your requests don't seem as important anymore. People drawing close to God realize that it's not just that he gives the answers; he *is* the answer. I found Bill Hybels'

---

1. This is one reason I don't like the term "spiritual disciplines." Maybe it's just me, but a discipline sounds like something I do and has overtones of work. I think the means of growth are ways to receive grace.

suggestion very helpful: write out why you are thankful to God and what you admire about him in the form of a written prayer. Jesus taught to start prayer with "Our father in heaven, may your name be honored,"—in other words, begin by reviewing God's father love, dwelling on his glory. Writing helps keep your mind from wandering.

If you're not feeling grateful for anything, it's *even more important* that you not move on until you break through with real thanksgiving. Unless we assume our correct place before God, no good prayer is possible. This is the part where you are presenting yourself to God as one alive from the dead.

If you get regular in a morning time with God, your other times of prayer will go better all day long. I can't stress too strongly the need for regularity. If you only have ten minutes, start there. You will soon begin to look forward to this time and find ways to expand it.

Author Ole Hallesby cites Revelation 3:20: "I stand at the door and knock; if anyone hears my voice and opens the door, I will come in to him, and will dine with him, and he with me." Hallesby says this verse is a good description of prayer, because prayer is letting Jesus enter our lives, our minds, and our situations.

That's why we can pray not only with words, but in silence. David urges us, "Rest [or 'be silent'] in the Lord and wait patiently for Him" (Psalms 37:7). He also says, "My soul waits in silence for God only; from him is my salvation. He only is my rock and my salvation, my stronghold; I shall not be greatly shaken" (Psalms 62:1-2). One of the great experiences we hope to have while praying is hearing or sensing God speaking to us.

When God speaks, it's usually not in words. Rather, you will sense him impressing you with something—not infrequently, with his love and near-ness to you. To stand silently before God is not as easy as it sounds. We prefer talking to listening. Try devoting part of your regular time to simply standing (figuratively) openly and silently before your loving father. See what happens.

Intercessory prayer, or prayer for others, is good, and brings our relationships into the picture. We'll see how God can use this aspect of prayer in an upcoming chapter.

THE ATTITUDE OF PRAYER

In addition to your set times, you can set your minds on the things of the Spirit by simply turning directly to God in your heart at any time during the day. Like turning over a mental leaf, you easily bring God into your thoughts by turning your mental "face" toward him. What matters in these times isn't so much what you say, but the fact that you form the intent to interact directly with him.

At other times, you may simply remember that God is with you as you do your work, drive, interact with others, or have lunch. David says, "I know the Lord is always with me. I will not be shaken, for he is right beside me" (Psalms 16:8). Jesus is right beside you all day long, and the more you acknowledge that, the better. As you remember God, you will be setting your mind on the things of the spirit as you let him into your affairs.

LEARNING THE VERTICAL PERSPECTIVE

People in our world go through their days pursuing goals, fending off problems, interacting with others, and a million other things. When going through each day, an important question is whether we are simply reacting to what is happening around us in sort of an automatic way, or whether we are actively bringing the spiritual mindset to bear on our lives through prayer.

A big part of prayer is coming to God continually for help interpreting your world. You could just react: "I can't believe she just said that! She's a real...." This is the horizontal perspective. God wants us to learn to look at our lives vertically as well as horizontally. When your friend says that mean thing, you could either spend your time reflecting on how bad she is, or you could step back mentally from the conflict and ask, "God, what are you trying to do here? What do you want me to see?"

When you do this, you are considering your daily life from God's perspective. You are interpreting your experience theo-centrically (with God at the center) instead of anthro-centrically (with man at the center). This is what Proverbs 3:6 means when it says, "In all your ways acknowledge Him, and He will direct your paths." Acknowledging God in our daily interactions—adopting the vertical perspective—is a large part of what it means to walk according to the Spirit.

Have you ever felt a smile spread across your face as you realize the truth of God dawning on your darkened and angry heart? It can be downright embarrassing at times to realize how far we have been from God's perspective in our daily struggles. At times I have shuddered in embarrassment when I realized I've been struggling for hours or even days on the horizontal axis without even considering what God is doing. If this happens to you, it's pointless to engage in a session of self-flagellation. Just immediately bring God back into your thought life.

God doesn't always explain what's happening, maybe even for a long time. But anyone who is abiding in prayerful desire to learn God's view is minding the things of the Spirit, and this will result in blessing.

The Spirit will call on us to cooperate actively in every situation as he shows us his mind. But only those who are prepared to heed spiritual things will ever grasp his teaching.

GETTING OUTSIDE OURSELVES

One of the biggest barriers to direct fellowship with God is our inability to get outside ourselves. I knew a guy who couldn't stop talking about himself long enough to relate to other people. No matter how hard I tried, I always had the feeling that he had not listened to a thing I said, because he just kept endlessly talking about himself. As you can imagine, this guy had a lot of problems with relationships. In fact, he was incapable of developing a friendship. Many times I have listened to him go on about all his strange and varied hobbies and preoccupations, mentally shaking my head in dismay, wondering how I could help him. I often tried to explain the problem to him, but he didn't get it.

This must be the way God feels when he listens to some of us pray. We can't get outside of ourselves and into him. We are turning to him, supposedly for a period of personal relating, but all we can think of or talk about is ourselves, our problems, our desires, our conflicts, our disappointments, and our failures. Of course, there is a place for talking about all these things. But when our prayer is a self-centered monologue, all elements of personal relationship are lost.

Most people thought my self-absorbed friend was annoying. At least with God we don't have to worry about that. His patience is infinite. But we do suffer when we come to God self-absorbed; we are blocking normal relationship. We are filling both sides of the relationship with one person: me. No wonder we often come away from a time of prayer with the sense we weren't able to draw close to God!

God wants us to draw close to him with confidence (Hebrews 4:16), but to do so, we have to stop thinking about ourselves long enough to get into him.

LEGALISTIC AND FORMALISTIC VERSIONS OF PRAYER

What does prayer look like under the legalistic mentality? One of the clearest warning signs is the presence of the twin brother to legalism: formalism.

Formalism is an outlook that focuses on outward religious rites more than inward heart attitudes. Just as legalism seeks to reform the inward by focusing on outward behavior, formalism ignores the inward in order to focus on things such as rituals and observance of sacred calendars and liturgies. Of course, every Christian group has forms through which people express their faith, and all of these forms have the potential to replace a real heart encounter with God.

Many religions, including some that would call themselves Christian, are deeply mired in formalistic prayer. Instead of a time of personal relating with God, prayer has become a ritual, a form to be followed. Just as you have to push a succession of buttons to get your money from an automatic teller machine, you have to follow various sequences of prayer disciplines to get your blessing from God. These external actions often do not correspond to anything going on inside.

Sometimes, people don't even bother to speak their own words, but instead let religious leaders write their prayers for them. This must have been the case when God uttered one of his clearest rejections of formalism in Isaiah 29:13-14:

> Because this people draw near with their words
> And honor Me with their lip service,
> But they remove their hearts far from Me,
> And their reverence for Me consists of tradition learned by rote…
> And the wisdom of their wise men shall perish.

People are the same today as they were then. The religious mind likes to recite outward forms and formulas "learned by rote." That way, they don't need to put out the effort involved in personal relating.

When people become formalistic, they conclude that a certain sequence of words is what matters rather than the intent of their hearts. It may be that people sometimes focus intently on the meaning of a memorized prayer, or one that is written in advance. But we don't relate to other persons this way. The danger of formalism is high when we are not spontaneously and naturally communicating to God, but relying instead on prewritten or memorized prayers.

In some religious groups, you can buy prayers with money. Religious functionaries can be hired to repeat a prayer on someone else's behalf for a certain fee, even if that other person is already dead! Yet Jesus taught against meaningless repetition in prayer (Matthew 6:7-8).

In some Buddhist sects, worshippers can spin prayer wheels as they enter a shrine. As the wheel spins, a printed prayer passes by a stylus, thus repeating the prayer over and over. Some worshippers use a hand-held, portable version that spins like a toy. In this extreme type of formalism we see clearly a machine-like image of prayer, and by implication, of God. These extreme examples of formalism help us see the problem but they are only different in degree from that we might engage in as Christians.

People wonder why God prescribed formalized worship in the Old Testament if formalism is bad. The main answer is that the forms in the Old Testament symbolically prefigured the work of Christ. These symbolic acts were for teaching. The New Testament dramatically reduces forms and rituals. Further, the New Testament warns believers against returning to the Old Testament forms, because they are now inappropriate for people living in the fulfillment of those symbols, with direct access to God (Colossians 2:16-23; Hebrews 8-10).

Any of us might lapse into formalistic prayer if we fail to consciously resist it. Sometimes the line between formalism and reality in spiritual things is difficult to detect, and seeing it requires spiritual sensitivity.

Let's take a couple of examples. Many Christians find it helpful to have a short time of prayer before meals. First thing in the morning is another popular time for prayer, as is "when I lay me down to sleep." These regular parts of our day can serve as reminders to pray, and we are creatures of habit. Could these times also become formalistic? How would we know if they had?

The mere fact that we pray at regular times doesn't mean we are formalists. To issue such a verdict would be to ironically focus once more on the external. But formalism is not a matter of the outward. It's an inward state of mind—an attitude. To determine whether such practices are formalistic, we need to look deeper.

Why is formalism objectionable? Simply put, formalism is impersonal. Formalists can go through their motions without ever addressing God personally. Therefore, we could pray at regular times like these without being formalistic, but if we find we are not making personal inward contact with God—if we don't really face him, but just rattle off words—then we are probably practicing formalism. We should avoid this at all times, because it's a negative habit.

Imagine someone entering your living room and reading out a prewritten statement before turning and leaving. Is this a personal interaction? Suppose your neighbor stops by your house before eating each meal, sticks his head in your door and rattles off the same few words before closing the door and leaving. Would this be personal communication? It might be, if you had dropped off a meal for him and he was just stopping by to thank you for it. But clearly it might not be personal, especially if he did it every day at the same time. Formalism is truly an inward attitude, not an outward action.

Sometimes we mouth words of prayer at appropriate times without any thought whatsoever. When we are formalistic, we, like any legalist, can tell ourselves we have prayed several times that day, so all is well. Whether there's any personal reality to our prayer lives is another question entirely.

Turn away from formalism! Always view your times of prayer as intensely personal times of communication and communion with a personal God who loves you.

WHY PERSISTENT PRAYER?

The New Testament teaches that we should be persistent in prayer. This means we should continue to pray over a period of time until God answers, particularly if we know what are praying for is his will. This used to stumble me as a young Christian because I thought it favored formalism. I used to wonder, can't God hear a request the first time? Wouldn't it demonstrate more faith if we just asked once, trusting that he had heard, and never mentioned it again?

It turns out that the answer is no. God says it demonstrates more faith if we come back to him regularly with our requests. By insisting that we pray persistently, God teaches us to spend more time with him.

Jesus taught on the need for persistent prayer in Luke 18. Luke records, "He was telling them a parable to show that at all times they ought to pray and not to lose heart" (v. 1). Then he told the following confusing parable:

> There was in a certain city a judge who did not fear God, and did not respect man. And there was a widow in that city, and she kept coming to him, saying, "Give me legal protection from my opponent." And for a while he was unwilling; but afterward he said to himself, "Even though I do not fear God nor respect man, yet because this widow bothers me, I will give her legal protection, lest by continually coming she wear me out." And the Lord said, "Hear what the unrighteous judge said; now shall not God bring about justice for His elect, who cry to Him day and night, and will He delay long over them?" (Luke 18:2-7)

This parable is baffling to many modern readers. How could Jesus compare this episode with an unrighteous judge to prayer? The judge's motive was avoiding harassment, not love. How should we interpret this parable? Is it saying we should pray until we annoy God so much that he grants our requests?

The problem is that this parable (like some others) uses a form of argument popular at the time but rarely used today. The argument is called an *a fortiori* argument, which is different from arguments by analogy that we usually use today. In an analogy, you compare two things for similarity, with the idea that if they are similar in one area, they should be similar in another. The parts of the comparison need to match fairly well for the analogy to be convincing.

In an *a fortiori* argument, one part of the comparison is similar, and one part is different. The similar part should match well, but the different part has to be as different as possible to make the argument convincing. The form of the argument is, "If this, how much more that?"

Let's look at the parable of the unrighteous judge in a diagram.

The woman's persistent request	Our persistence in prayer	Similar
The judge's motives for answering	God's motives for answering	Different

Jesus even calls the judge "unrighteous," so he is not saying the judge and God are alike. On the contrary, the fact that they are so different makes us realize if this no-good judge would answer her, how much more will our loving father answer us?

Why does God call us to persist in prayer? He is omniscient, so he already knows what we will ask. He is omnipotent, so he is able to answer the first time we ask. Yet he wants us to persist. Why? The answer is that persistence is not for God's sake, but ours. Our reluctance to pray is one reason. He knows we would not spend the time we need with him if he didn't withhold answers for a period of time. Then, after persistent prayer, the answer comes. As a result, our faith is strengthened and we learn to keep praying.

IS IT MY DUTY TO EAT DINNER?

We need to view prayer as more than a duty or a chance to ask for things. Prayer is also one of the main ways we set our minds on the things of the Spirit.

Eating food is not something we normally view as a duty. It tastes good, feels good, and is essential for healthy living. Why view it as a duty when it's one of the pleasures of life? It's the same with prayer. If prayer is so burdensome that we view it as a duty, it usually means we are coming to God under law, or in Adam.

There may be times when we are so busy or preoccupied that it takes a conscious act of the will, even a struggle, before we can enter into meaningful prayer. When this is the case, we can go ahead and do the right thing, depending on God's power to do so. Very quickly, we will be glad we did.

CONCLUSION

Our discussion of prayer is not over. We can't have full understanding of prayer without considering how it interacts with other aspects of our spiritual lives. The following chart considers some of the connections between prayer and the other means of growth.

THE INTERACTION BETWEEN PRAYER AND OTHER MEANS OF GROWTH

| FELLOWSHIP | Jesus gave corporate prayer a special place when he said, "If two of you agree on earth about anything that they may ask, it shall be done for them by My Father who is in heaven" (Matthew 18:19). Jesus is implying here that corporate prayer is more powerful than individual prayer, if only because when two or more agree, they are more likely to have correctly discerned the will of God. A church's prayer ministry is one of its most important. Corporate prayer is also an opportunity to build one another up. |

MINISTRY

A ministry weak in prayer will tend to be overly dependent on human effort. What we cannot accomplish via the power of God, we will try to supply through our own strength. Such groups are tempted to use force, manipulation, and compulsion on people to secure action. If God blessed such a ministry, it would only encourage more of the same, and it would result in pride. So God's power is blocked. When people in ministry truly come to appreciate the power of prayer and come together frequently to pray, their faith releases God's power into ministry situations. Another key area where prayer intersects with ministry is spiritual warfare. To tear down Satan's fortresses, prayer is essential. Without it, he consistently has success resisting the people of God.

SCRIPTURE

We need to pray that God will take scriptural truth and apply it to our lives in a living way. Also, if we have learned the scriptures in good measure, God will call biblical statements to mind in order to bring us understanding about what he is doing in our daily lives. Communication from God through scripture never has to be questioned like more subjective forms of communication do.

DISCIPLINE OF THE HOLY SPIRIT

Cultivating the vertical perspective through abiding in Christ is a prerequisite for much of the Lord's discipline to be effective. As we shall see later, those who will not take their trials to God in prayer—not just asking that the trial would go away, but seeking to understand what God is teaching—will not benefit from the suffering they undergo. Thanksgiving during trial is crucial to gaining all that God has for us in the trial.

WALKING ACCORDING TO THE SPIRIT: SCRIPTURE

How do we "set our minds on the things of the Spirit?" One important way is through the Bible. Nothing is more of a "thing of the Spirit" than scripture. The Holy Spirit moved prophets to write every part of it (2 Peter 1:21). By deepening your knowledge and love of scripture, you open the best possible pathway to hear from God. Also, the supernatural transforming power of the word can change you in mysterious ways.

OUR PRIVILEGE

The human race has been uniquely blessed by God. For us Christ was incarnated and died. But that's not all. God has also given us something more precious than money or fame. He has given us his word.

Imagine an alien spaceship landing somewhere in a city. Thousands of people gather around the ship just like in the old science fiction movies. Finally the aliens emerge—strange creatures, very advanced. "We have come to answer your questions," they announce. "This is a book explaining our world and much of what we know about history, science, and more." Then they take off, leaving the book behind. Wouldn't that be an interesting book? People would line up for a chance to read and understand such a book.

But what we have is much better than any book imaginary aliens could possibly leave us. We have thoughts from the creator of the universe. We have the history of his dealings with the human race. We have the Bible.

Considering how important the Bible is, it's surprising how little many believers have learned about it. Studies of western Christians show convincingly that real biblical understanding is at historic lows. For real spiritual growth, a churchy knowledge of Bible stories won't do. To set our minds on the things of the spirit through scripture, we need a deeper kind of knowledge.

SPIRITUAL GROWTH WITHOUT THE BIBLE?

Peter tells his readers, "Like newborn babes, long for the pure milk of the word, that by it you may grow in respect to salvation" (1 Peter 2:2). Neglecting to learn the word of God will always eventually result in a complete stunting of spiritual growth, according to Paul. In 1 Corinthians 3:1-2, he recalls to the Corinthians that he could not speak to them "as to spiritual men, but as to men of flesh, as to babes in Christ." Therefore, he gave them the food of babies. "I gave you milk to drink, not solid food; for you were not yet able to receive it. Indeed, even now you are not yet able." The last phrase stands as a warning. Sadly, we may be years old as Christians but still babies spiritually. One way to know we are spiritual babies is when we cannot digest the meat of the word. We are still living on milk. Hebrews 5:12-6:1 says:

> For though by this time you ought to be teachers, you have need again for someone to teach you the elementary principles of the oracles of God, and you have come to need milk and not solid food. For everyone who partakes only of milk is not accustomed to the word of righteousness, for he is a babe. But solid food is for the mature, who because of practice have their senses trained to discern good and evil. Therefore leaving the elementary teaching about the Christ, let us press on to maturity.

You see that it says, "Whoever partakes only of milk is not accustomed to the word of righteousness." In other words, they don't know their Bibles. If we think we are going to mature without ever learning the Bible, we have a surprise coming. According to these passages, there is no such thing as a mature Christian who is "not accustomed to the word of righteousness." No amount of prayer, fellowship, or spiritual experience can make up for a deficient knowledge of God's word.

THE USE OF SCRIPTURE IN MINISTRY

Today, the western church seeks to promote evangelism and spiritual growth, but our approach often approximates Madison Avenue more than the New Testament. As a result, evangelism is ineffective or people fade away soon after their profession of faith. A church without a strong ministry of the word is reduced to holding a side show to attract the attention of unmotivated believers. Pastors and leaders are left wondering how much real maturity their people have.

A key difference between many of our ministries today and the early church is that they relied more heavily on the power of the scriptures. Paul called on the members (not just the leaders) of the church in Colossae to learn their Bibles: "Let the word of Christ richly dwell within you" (Colossians 3:16). This would rarely be a good description of the level of Bible knowledge in modern western churches.

In 2 Timothy 3:16 he tells Timothy, "All scripture is inspired by God and profitable for teaching, for reproof, for correction, for training in righteousness; that the man of God may be adequate, equipped for every good work." Although many in the modern world of Christianity may feel they have found a better way, God still thinks his word is the tool of choice for Christian ministry. Paul goes on to adjure Timothy:

> Preach the word...with great patience and instruction... for the time will come when they will not endure sound doctrine; but wanting to have their ears tickled, they will accumulate for themselves teachers in accordance to their own desires; and will turn away their ears from the truth, and will turn aside to myths.
> (2 Timothy 4:1-4)

Today, as then, Christians would often rather hear sensational stories about miracles and witches than clear teaching of God's word. But those of us with a burden for building others up in Christ should, like Timothy, focus on sharing the word of God.

SPIRITUAL WARFARE AND THE BIBLE

The Bible is also essential in our spiritual growth because of spiritual warfare. To oppose the Evil One we need every spiritual weapon God has provided for us. When Paul describes the weapons of spiritual warfare, he refers to the word of God, in one form or another, more than any other thing. Can you pick out three separate items of armor in this passage that refer to the word of God?

> Therefore, take up the full armor of God, that you may be able
> to resist in the evil day, and having done everything, to stand
> firm. Stand firm therefore, having girded your loins with truth,
> and having put on the breastplate of righteousness, and having
> shod your feet with the preparation of the gospel of peace;
> in addition to all, taking up the shield of faith with which you
> will be able to extinguish all the flaming missiles of the evil one.
> And take the helmet of salvation, and the sword of the Spirit,
> which is the word of God. (Ephesians 6:13-17)

The loin girdle of "truth," the shoes, which are the "preparation of the gospel of peace," and, of course, the sword of the Spirit, "which is the word of God," all refer to the Bible. No other thing is mentioned as often in this list.

If we plan to step up and oppose Satan, we had better be able to handle the word of God like Jesus did when he fought the devil in Luke 4:1-13. Every time Satan challenged Jesus to sin, Jesus replied with the formula, "It is written…." Are we able to fight with the devil this way? Some of us are vulnerable because we don't know the Bible well enough to meet his attacks effectively.

THE BIBLE UNDER THE LEGALISTIC PARADIGM

I once went to speak at a retreat for a small fundamentalist church with a friend of mine who had grown up in that church but had long since moved to another city. That Friday evening I gave an impassioned plea for spiritual growth from Romans 6. Afterward, I threw the floor open for discussion, anticipating some good challenging interaction from the small group of two dozen college and career-aged believers. The first guy raised his hand, and I called on him. "Uh, yeah, what's your view on predestination?" he asked.

I recoiled in shock. I hadn't spoken a word on the subject of election or anything related to it. This guy seemed like he hadn't been listening! Politely, I sketched out my position in a couple of minutes and looked to the others for discussion on growing in Christ. Another guy raised his hand. "Do you believe in eternal security?"

Again, I had to strain to keep my eyes from bulging too much in surprise. Why were they asking me questions that were off the subject? Had my lecture been so uninteresting? The rest of the discussion continued to turn on similar controversial questions, never returning to the notion of growth. Later, as we drove home, I commented to my friend about the odd lines of questioning we got. He chuckled and said he remembered when growing up that those subjects had come up in that group almost every week.

What was this happening? I have been in numerous situations before and since in which the same thing transpired. Instead of discussing something that mattered, we always seemed to end up discussing whether Hell is conscious or whether there are more than three levels in Heaven. Predestination and eternal security are favorites.

This is what we might call doctrinal wrangling. It's similar to "straining out the gnat and swallowing the camel." As discussed earlier, straining out the gnat is when people focus on minor moral imperatives in order to divert attention from moral failure in important areas. The practice of doctrinal wrangling accomplishes the same thing in the area of truth. Both groups and individuals practice it. Rather than face the stark reality of God's truth, the doctrinal wrangler can have a sporting debate while never having to seriously consider changing in his life based on the claims of the word of God.

Of course Heaven and predestination can be important topics in the right context. But when they are foils, designed to turn aside the sword of God's word, such discussions take on an ugly, almost obscene appearance.

Why divert attention from what God is trying to say? Usually the reason is legalism. Only a legalist feels the need to keep the subject on "safe" topics, because only the legalist is in danger of accusation from the Bible. Believers under grace might confront their need to change, but that won't be a problem, because they are able to admit wrong without feeling their identities are being threatened.

JESUS AND DOCTRINAL WRANGLING

During Jesus' ministry, law-living people tried to engage him in meaningless prattle about what is permitted under law and what is not. We hear his exasperation when he addresses one of these silly discussions in Matthew 23:16-17:

> Woe to you, blind guides, who say, "Whoever swears by the temple, that is nothing; but whoever swears by the gold of the

temple, he is obligated." You fools and blind men; which is more important, the gold, or the temple that sanctified the gold?

Someone at the retreat I mentioned earlier might have asked, "Well, which is it, the gold or the temple?" The answer should be obvious. This whole line of thought is so stupid that it's amazing anyone would ever waste even a minute on it! "You fools and blind men," Jesus cries. How could they be taking the spiritual discussion in Israel in this direction when they needed to address real issues?

Legalism will invariably have a deadening effect on our knowledge of the Bible. We end up with a sort of knowledge, but it cannot give life. Some of us raised in evangelical churches know who Zerubbabel was, but we can't recognize a balanced position from an imbalanced one. Some of us know James 2:14 by heart, but we couldn't bring out our Bibles and use them in real evangelistic or counseling situations if our lives depended on it.

A RELIGIOUS TEXT OR A PERSONAL LETTER?

Formalism in the use of scripture is another manifestation of legalism. Any time we only read or recite the Bible for a feeling of blessing without taking the time to understand what it means, we are practicing formalism, which is a sign of legalism.

Other religions treat their scriptural texts formalistically. Most think the words themselves are sacred, not what they mean. They read and chant the words, often with no understanding. Some even recite their texts in a foreign language that nobody understands. Various religious traditions don't allow human hands to touch the text. Readers use a stylus to point to the words and turn the pages.

These tendencies are also present in the history of Christianity. Formalism has a rich history in Christianity, with the older traditions leading the way. For centuries, the Bible was unavailable to the public because the Latin Vulgate version was considered the only one sanctioned by God. Was God able to learn Latin, but unable to learn German or French?

Newer churches have also shown little resistance to formalism at times. For instance, some groups refuse to do critical and background study, insisting on taking the words as they are off the page. Some extreme fundamental churches refuse to accept any translation other than the *King James Version*. One sister defended her loyalty to the *King James Version* to me by saying, "If it was good enough for Paul and Peter, it's good enough for me!"

Formalism takes the meaning and depth out of scripture and replaces them with repetition and outward readings that do not penetrate into our minds and spirits.

INTERPRETATION: THE FIRST STEP

Some extremist groups believe that studying scripture is unspiritual. Instead, they engage in "prayer reading." They just read verses over and over again while moaning and calling on God to apply the verse. By never discussing the meaning of the passage, they believe they are bypassing the "natural understanding" stage, and going directly to the "spiritual understanding" stage.

How wrong this approach is! The Bible is a book of *propositional truth*, which means passages should be analyzed for their meaning. We have to be prepared to study the context and thought development of each passage we want to understand. Information about the author and original audience could affect the meaning. We should be able to use language helps to understand vocabulary and grammar. Historical and critical tools available today (including good Bible software) make even the typical English speaker fully adequate to interpret all but the most difficult passages.

Finally, we have to consider the meaning we get from a passage in the light of our overall understanding of scripture. If we believe that God has inspired the whole Bible, we should never take statements in isolation. Rather, we should consider how they fit into everything the Bible says about that topic. The best protection God has given us against incorrect Bible interpretation is the rest of the Bible.

Every teacher of false doctrine can quote Bible verses to back up his imbalanced position. But those who know the whole counsel of God will quickly see through misuse of proof texts. There can be no shortcut to authentic biblical understanding.

WHERE DO I START?

If you want to experience the full power available through the Bible, you need to accept the importance of personal Bible study (2 Timothy 2:15). How far must you go in studying the Bible to feel secure that you are not unarmed in your struggle? I suggest you must at least get to the point where you are a *self-starter* in the word. A self-starter is one who can pick up the Bible and know how to evaluate most passages in it. A self-starter is able to assess an argument by a Bible teacher, evaluating the value, accuracy, and balance of his argument.

To get this type of reliable understanding of scripture, we need to study using sound principles of interpretation. You can learn these principles from books like *How to Read the Bible for All Its Worth* by Gordon Fee and Douglas Stuart, or *Protestant Biblical Interpretation* by Bernard Ramm.

You'll need a modern translation of the Bible so you don't have trouble with the language, and you really need more than one so you can compare translations. That's a great way to pick up semantic range—the range of possible readings. You'll also need some tools to help you understand the language and the cultural context of the text. A Christian bookstore manager will be able to suggest Bible study guides that are interesting and helpful.

If you use commentaries or study Bibles with explanations, remember that each one is the opinion of one person. The best way to use them is to have several, and compare their arguments. You'll quickly see they often don't agree with each other, so they are not infallible.

MEDITATION

Once we have done the study and are satisfied with our interpretation of a text, the next step is meditation. Meditation means we reflect on how a given truth applies to our own or others' lives. One of the top advocates for meditation on scripture is David:

> How blessed is the man whose delight is in the torah of the Lord,
> And in His torah he meditates day and night.
> (Psalms 1:1-3)

> When I remember You on my bed,
> I meditate on You in the night watches.
> (Psalms 63:6)

God told Joshua, "This book of the torah shall not depart from your mouth, but you shall meditate on it day and night..." (Joshua 1:7-8). Meditation is the process of making biblical truth part of your own thinking.

A great aid to meditation is to memorize key sections of the text you are studying. That way, you can think about the passage when you don't have a Bible open. Memorized scripture is also helpful because God uses memorized passages like a spiritual vocabulary to communicate to you.

In meditation, you prayerfully ask God to take you deeper into the meaning of the text. You watch for situations in real life that resemble what you read. You ponder the relationships between a particular passage and other things you've read in scripture. You think of people you know who might benefit from the passage.

Focus first on how you could apply the passage to your own life. God may immediately shed light on an area of your life that needs attention. He may show you ways to improve important relationships, or where you have wronged someone and need to change your attitude. He will also encourage you by reminding you of things like his love and answers to prayer.

TRUTH AND EXPERIENCE

Both truth and personal experience are important in the Christian life. However, they are not equal. God says we should understand in light of the truth. For instance, we are told to be anxious for nothing (Philippians 4:6). In other words, when our feelings are telling us to be scared, God says we should overrule our feeling state with the truth that he will care for us.

The same must be true with the feeling of desire. Desire for something can be a real and strong emotional experience. But God refers to some desires as "evil" (Colossians 3:5). This is only one of many such statements in scripture. We often misinterpret our experiences unless our thinking is deeply steeped in God's word. We need an objective authority by which to judge our feelings, experiences, and circumstances because such things are subjective and unreliable as a guide to life.

Have you ever felt like someone was angry at you, only to find out later you were wrong? Our feelings and impressions are often in error because our feelings are fallen, just like our thoughts. We can't assume that everything we think is automatically right, and neither should we believe that everything we feel is necessarily right.

We live in an age that is increasingly losing the distinction between feelings and truth. In our culture, even reality itself has to answer to the feelings and impressions of the individual. The question is no longer, "Is it true?" but "Does it work for you?" Though such feelings and impressions may be in contradiction from one person to another, that's no problem. We just conclude that different people have different realities! The most important thing, according to the modern world, is to follow our feelings—to be true to ourselves.

Maturing in the Lord means learning to distrust our perceptions, at least to the extent that we compare and submit our perceptions to what God says. Refusal to do this constitutes a form of arrogance that can effectively block spiritual growth. If we always think our feelings are the truth, we are not in a position to hear a different point of view from God. We become very headstrong and hard to lead.

Counselors today are worried that Christians will deny or ignore their feelings because they believe such feelings are wrong. This is a valid concern. We have no need to deny or ignore anything. The point is not to deny, but to critique. And we cannot critique our feelings unless we acknowledge them. On the other hand, if we are not prepared to critique our perceptions and feelings, then our feelings have become the true integration point of our lives, rather than God and his word

THE BIBLE AND THE OTHER MEANS OF GROWTH

There are several means of growth, and all of them interact with each other. The word is particularly important in correctly understanding and practicing the other means of growth. The following chart details various means of growth and the way in which our use of each is impacted by scripture. Of course we should also remember that we wouldn't even know about the other means of growth without the Bible.

HOW THE WORD OF GOD INTERACTS WITH THE OTHER MEANS OF GROWTH	
PRAYER	In our prayer life, the Bible provides the proper basis for knowing God's will. John says that praying according to God's will is a condition for being answered: "If we ask anything according to His will, He hears us. And if we know that He hears us in whatever we ask, we know that we have the requests which we have asked from Him" (I John 5:14). Jesus also taught that effective prayer is based on the word (John 15:7). This is a powerful promise, but it is conditional. Also, when praying against Satan, we need to cite our authority from the word like Jesus did.

MINISTRY

Servanthood is a means of growth, but effective service involves "speaking the truth in love" (Ephesians 4:15). No ministry will have the power God wants it to have unless the one ministering is powerful in the word of God. Even service ministers who may not teach or preach need the wisdom available through God's word. If you want to see people's lives change show them how to get into the word.

BODY LIFE

The basis for Christian fellowship is not only love but truth. The Body of Christ is a community of truth, and these two can never be separated. In Philippians 1:9-10 Paul prays "that your love may abound still more and more in real knowledge and all discernment, so that you may approve the things that are excellent, in order to be sincere and blameless until the day of Christ." Truth is the framework that makes real love possible. This is why we are called on to "speak the truth in love" to one another (Ephesians 4:15).

DISCIPLINE OF THE HOLY SPIRIT

The discipline of the Holy Spirit is a means of growth, but it won't be effective unless we interpret our trials appropriately. We need scripture like Hebrews 12 to teach us how to respond to discipline in a way that promotes growth. When our feelings are pulling us down during suffering, the word becomes an anchor that gives us stability and faith.

Unless we see all the means of growth as an interconnected plan for God's provision, we will miss his plan for our lives. The word of God takes its place at the center of that plan.

WALKING ACCORDING TO THE SPIRIT: FELLOWSHIP

In Christianity, we "set our minds on the things of the Spirit" corporately, not just individually. Other religions usually offer the option of personal spiritual advancement apart from other people, but not Christianity. God gives Christians only one option if we want maturity: spiritual growth in the context of Christian community.

God doesn't tell us exactly why he decided to set it up so that we have to depend on others, but he did it. Maybe he didn't want us to become arrogant, thinking we are strong enough in ourselves to grow apart from others. Maybe he felt we would be safer from the enemy if we stick together. Maybe he felt we needed a curb on selfishness. The centrality of love in the Christian ethic also accords well with holding fellowship as essential.

One thing is clear: God intends Christians to come together as a group regularly and to build into each other's lives so we can grow. According to D. A. Carson, when the New Testament supplies reason-clauses for why the church assembled, it never gives worship as the reason. Instead, the reason we meet is to build up the body of Christ.[1]

---

1. D. A. Carson, "Worship Under the Word" in D. A. Carson, Ed. *Worship by the Book*, (Grand Rapids: Zondervan, 2002), 25.

KOINONIA

The New Testament always presents Christians as a community, no matter what the locality. Christians are to assemble and build into each other's lives, sharing the common life of God with one another. This sharing is called *koinonia* in the New Testament. This is a rich word, often translated "fellowship," but with more meaning than our word fellowship conveys. *Koinonia* suggests an exchange of something. It literally means to have in common, or to share. Through sharing the common life of Jesus with each other in fellowship, we effectively set our minds on the things of the Spirit.

The New Testament describes Christians using their spiritual gifts and relationships to build one another up. Koinonia is therefore a powerful means of growth. The word "church" (*ekklesia*) means an assembly, or a group, so you don't need to join a conventional or "official" church to experience fellowship. The important thing is to find a group of fellow Christians where you can join together in this project.

As you ponder your friends in the body of Christ, looking to God for ways to build them up, you are setting your minds on the things of the Spirit. Quality body life will take up a sizeable portion of your thought life, and this is all part of the spiritual mindset involved in walking according to the Spirit. Indeed, focusing on how to give out to others is the best kind of spiritual thought life—focused on others rather than just on self.

Unfortunately, the experience of "going to church" in the modern world may have little in common with what the New Testament teaches about *koinonia*. If you are already in a church you feel good about, you should seek opportunities to deepen your involvement in real *koinonia*, probably in the context of a smaller group.

An in-depth study of all the passages dealing with the church would be beyond the scope of this book. But if you are not already familiar with basic passages on Christian fellowship, take a minute to study the following chart that contains some of the relevant biblical data.

FELLOWSHIP AS A MEANS OF GROWTH

1 CORINTHIANS 12:21
And the eye cannot say to the hand, "I have no need of you"; or again the head to the feet, "I have no need of you."

No Christian should claim he or she doesn't need ministry from and to other believers. The context of this statement makes it clear that we have all been given gifts for the edification of others. By implication, if we cannot say we don't need them, they cannot say they don't need us! Notice that it's not just the presence of the other members that we need, but also their functions.

1 CORINTHIANS 12:7, 14
But to each one is given the manifestation of the Spirit for the common good ... For the body is not one member, but many.

Our gifts are for the common good, i.e., for the good of others. Because we are a part, and not the whole, of the Body of Christ, we need what the other parts of the Body supply. God has not gifted any of us so much that we can meet all our own needs.

1 CORINTHIANS 14:26
What is the outcome then, brethren? When you assemble, each one has a psalm, has a teaching, has a revelation, has a tongue, has an interpretation. Let all things be done for edification.

Our times of assembly together are for mutual edification (a word that means "to build up"). Whatever you believe about spiritual gifts, there can be no doubt that our meetings are for this purpose. Therefore, if we fail to assemble, we will miss out on edification.

EPHESIANS 4:15
Speaking the truth in love, we are to grow up in all aspects into Him who is the Head, even Christ.

The Body of Christ should be seen as an organic union based on genuine personal relationships and mutual interdependence. Within these relationships we have the opportunity to speak the truth in love. The important point is not just that we attend meetings (although this is a necessary aspect) but that we authentically share the life of Christ with one another.

HEBREWS 10:,24-25
Let us consider how to stimulate one another to love and good deeds, not forsaking our own assembling together, as is the habit of some, but encouraging one another; and all the more, as you see the day drawing near.

It is in the context of loving relationships that we can learn to stimulate each other to love and good deeds. Devoting time to our meetings is an essential part of this scenario.

ACTS 2:42,46
And they were continually devoting themselves to the apostles' teaching and to fellowship [koinonia], to the breaking of bread and to prayer... And day by day continuing with one mind in the temple, and breaking bread from house to house, they were taking their meals together with gladness and sincerity of heart.

The example of the early church included extensive involvement in fellowship. This fellowship included both large meetings (held at Solomon's portico, which was part of the temple), small meetings in homes, and informal times of social and spiritual relationship building. Their involvement was more or less daily according to this passage. Real koinonia means not just attendance at a meeting or two, but successfully building supportive relationships with the people of God.

ROMANS 12:4-6

For just as we have many members in one body and all the members do not have the same function, so we, who are many, are one body in Christ, and individually members one of another. And since we have gifts that differ according to the grace given to us, let each exercise them accordingly.

Our identity in Christ includes the aspect that we are "individually members of one another." This organic, spiritual, or mystical union of believers with Christ and each other is a sacred thing, which should be a dominant factor in our daily lives. We cannot ignore our union with other believers and still live out our new identity in Christ.

MATT. 18:19-20

Again I say to you, that if two of you agree on earth about anything that they may ask, it shall be done for them by My Father who is in heaven. For where two or three have gathered together in My name, there I am in their midst.

In this passage, Jesus puts special emphasis on his presence during times of Christian fellowship. It may be that some prayers will not be answered until we pray "Our Father," rather than "My Father."

1 CORINTHIANS 12:18

But now God has placed the members, each one of them, in the body, just as He desired.

The Body of Christ is constituted by God, not by man. A local manifestation of the Body of Christ can take different forms. One of these is an incorporated church. Whether a group is incorporated as a church or not, God recognizes all those who are united with Christ as members of his Body.

BARRIERS TO FELLOWSHIP

Some of us have had negative experiences in churches and find it hard to face the prospect of returning to something that hurt or bored us. But why let negative experiences that wounded you in the past continue to wound you in the present? There are different kinds of churches, and if one was negative, you should look for another.

We in the Western world have an additional barrier to fellowship: the extreme individualism of our culture. Traditional societies see much more easily the need for close community. In our society, Christians often move from city to city or within their own city, resulting in a weakened sense of community. Extreme individualistic ideas, like the view that our private lives are nobody else's business, are axiomatic in the west. Unfortunately, while we do have tons of privacy and nobody ever knows what is happening in our lives, we also suffer loneliness and a sense of emptiness as we live in a way were never designed to live.

The only way to minimize the negative impact of radical individualism for ourselves and our families is accept God's perspective. We will have to oppose our culture in this area, since its rampant individualism is simply incompatible with the biblical picture of community.

FELLOWSHIP UNDER THE LEGALISTIC PARADIGM

People with a legalistic mentality see "going to church" as a religious duty. Failure to observe the Lord's Day by missing church would cause the law-liver to feel guilty. But if this same law-oriented person attended church, he or she would feel good, even if no meaningful *koinonia* happened. Formalism rears its head in this area as it does with the other means of growth. To the formalist, the important thing is church membership and attendance at the service. Exchanging true ministry and building others up is optional.

Even when legalists feel obligated to minister in some fashion, the emphasis is on "putting in my time" rather than on true Christian love. Many churches cannot fill their own slots for volunteers even when they have already relegated most ministry to paid staff. The average western church is like a football game: twenty-two men on the field desperately in need of rest, while twenty thousand sit in the stands, desperately in need of exercise. The real source of this problem is formalism: the view that outward attendance is what matters rather than building relationships with and serving others, resulting in a real community of love.

This is not to say the church doesn't need organization, or that the outward features of local churches (buildings, pastors, classes, etc.) are wrong. The local church must organize its ministry if it is to be effective. The super-spiritual notion that people will spontaneously know and do the right thing is unbiblical. Church leaders should organize structures that facilitate ministry, including in-depth equipping (Ephesians 4:11-12).

Once we take the focus off of formalistic compliance to a legal standard of attendance and focus instead on the real issue—"faith working through love" (Galatians 5:6)—Christian fellowship becomes the means of growth it should be.

BODY LIFE AND THE OTHER MEANS OF GROWTH

Like all the means of growth, Christian fellowship interacts dynamically with the others. The following chart discusses some of these interactions.

THE INTERACTION OF FELLOWSHIP WITH THE OTHER MEANS OF GROWTH	
PRAYER	The church is to be a praying community. By precept and by example, prayer plays a central role in the life of the church. Others can stimulate us to love and good works (Hebrews 10:24-25), including prayer. By establishing regular times to pray with others, we can strengthen our prayer habits while gaining the discernment of the other members. Prayer is the spearhead of the church's ministry—opening doors, producing conviction in the hearts of those who hear, protecting those reached from Satan, and granting spiritual empowerment to Christian workers.
MINISTRY	The church exists to accomplish ministry, both to its members and to the world outside the church. If I do ministry off by myself, it's never as impactful as ministry accomplished with others. I need to learn to disciple (train) others so they can carry on the same kind of ministry. I may have to be disciplined myself before I can be effective at ministry, and this is best accomplished in a healthy local church.

SCRIPTURE	The church should teach the word of God. The church is ordered to equip its members to do the work of service (Ephesians 4:11-12). Instruction in the Bible is central to this commission. The church should also use the Bible to ground new Christians, and even for evangelism at its public meetings.
DISCIPLINE OF THE HOLY SPIRIT	When we undergo difficult times of spiritual discipline from the Lord, Christian fellowship is sometimes the only thing that keeps us from falling apart. We were never meant to undergo significant breaking without the support of a loving community. At the same time that I receive support, I have the opportunity to give support and to coach young Christians on how to understand God's hand in their lives during trials.

As the lines of the various means of growth converge toward a center, that center turns out to be the body of Christ.

WALKING ACCORDING TO THE SPIRIT: SERVING LOVE

Our beginning point in Romans 8 stressed how essential it is to "set our minds on the things of the Spirit." We can do this through prayer, Bible study, and Christian fellowship, as we have seen. In John 15, Jesus gives us yet another avenue for godly mental focus. He said, "I am the vine, you are the branches; he who abides in Me, and I in him, he bears much fruit; for apart from Me you can do nothing."

To abide in Christ includes a Christ-centered mental focus. If we have such a focus, He will bear fruit in us. But some of us have become fruit inspectors. We have lost our focus on the vine and have directed it to the fruit, which means having a performance-focus. Fruit is nice, and lack of fruit is unfortunate. But if we want more fruit, our focus needs to be on the vine, not on the fruit itself.

Jesus went on to further define what he meant by abiding in him. We have already seen part of this definition: "If you abide in Me, and My words abide in you, ask whatever you wish, and it shall be done for you." Both the word and prayer are first on Jesus' list. But he doesn't stop there.

In verse 9 he also says, "Just as the Father has loved Me, I have also loved you; abide in my love." So abiding in Jesus' love is also a part of what it means to abide in the vine. How do we "abide" in the love of Christ? He explains it for us:

> If you keep my commandments, you will abide in my love; just as
> I have kept my Father's commandments, and abide in His love...
> This is my commandment, that you love one another, just as I
> have loved you. Greater love has no one than this, that one lay
> down his life for his friends. [1] (John 15:10-13)

This passage teaches that self-giving love is one important way to set our minds on the things of the Spirit. We abide in the love of Jesus when we love one another as he loved us. Keeping Jesus' commands (the imperative) means specifically, in this passage, learning how to love others as he has loved us.

When Jesus said we should love "just as I have loved you," he signaled that he is not interested in the purely sentimental modern notion of love, but the self-sacrificial love he practiced. Let's look at a comparison between love as it is understood in the modern world and love as Jesus practiced it.

COMPARING BIBLICAL AND MODERN LOVE

MODERN LOVE	BIBLICAL LOVE
BASED ON EXPERIENCE Happens to a person when the "chemistry is right."	**BASED ON A DECISION** We can decide to invest ourselves in another by giving of ourselves to meet his or her needs. Jesus decided to die for us before we even existed (Ephesians 1:3)

---

1. I don't like translating *entole* as "commandment" in this passage. Giving commands is an activity associate in modern English with the military. Can you imagine giving your spouse, friend, or even your kids a list of your "commands"? Why not translate this passage, "This is my new instruction, or commission?" According to Kittel, the first usage for *entole* is "'to give a commission or direction' in general, and not specifically in the religious sense." *Theological Dictionary of the New Testament*, 2:545 (Grand Rapids, MI: Eerdmans, 1964-c1976).

DEFINED BY FEELING

"I love you" means I feel a certain warmth, desire, need, or affinity for you.

COMPATIBLE WITH FEELING

"I love you" may sometimes mean a feeling, but it always means a commitment to serve. Jesus may not have felt desire or warmth toward the soldiers who flogged him, but he died for them anyway.

CAN'T BE CONTROLLED

Love has to happen, so I can't be expected to choose to love someone. Therefore, love or lack of love is not a moral issue.

CAN BE CONTROLLED

Christian love is based on personal choice and commitment. Therefore, it is a moral issue (Mark 12:28-31).

DEPENDS ON THE OTHER PERSON

He or she must be attractive or lovely enough to elicit a love response in me.

DEPENDS ON GOD AND ME

I can love the unlovely, like Christ did when he died for us while we were enemies of God (Romans 5:10).

SELF-AFFIRMING

Love is a good feeling and needs to be two-way. If a relationship is not rewarding to me, I have the right to leave and find another.

SELF-SACRIFICIAL

Christian love is a commitment to give victoriously and keeps no record of whether the other person gives back (I Corinthians 13:5).

MEETS OTHERS' DESIRES

Effort is extended to please or pacify others by doing what they want.

MEETS OTHERS' NEEDS

Christian love is concerned with doing what is good for another, not with what the other wants. This love recognizes that what people want and what they need are often different. For example, the other person may need confrontation even if he or she doesn't want it.

LOVING OTHERS = GROWTH FOR ME

No growing Christian is surprised to discover that God wants us to learn to love others. But how does our giving love tie in with our own spiritual growth?

When God gives you success at building some relationships, you have the opportunity to practice self-giving love as you invest yourself into others. At that point, Christ-like love becomes a powerful means of growth. Your mind is set on the things of the Spirit as you work out with God how to build up your loved ones.

First, you come before God and reflect on the needs of your friends and family. Then, using your growing understanding of the word and how ministry works, you lay plans with God to meet those needs or to help others meet their own needs. You will likely sense God showing you things you can say and do for your loved ones. Both during this planning time and when you go to carry out your plans, you are setting your mind on the things of the Spirit.

Although you may not notice it right away, the power of the Holy Spirit is released into your life when you spend time thinking of others in an unselfish, spiritual way. You will grow through the insights God gives you during times of others-centered reflection and study. But there is much more. Since our mindset is more Christ-centered whenever we take our attention off ourselves and put it on God and others, it results in more spiritual health. Others-centered prayer and reflection bring a closeness to God that often evades us when we merely spend time with God thinking about ourselves.

God is concerned about the spiritual and personal needs of others, so as we orient our minds toward others, we adopt a perspective similar to God's own. Because we are moving in the same direction as God, we will be better able to move into his thoughts. Also, our desires and fears, which may cloud the water when thinking about ourselves, affect us less when we are thinking of others (unless it's a relationship where we are expecting something big for ourselves, like a romantic one).

LOSING MY LIFE FOR THE SAKE OF JESUS

Some Bible teachers are worried that Christians will think about their relationships with other people at the expense of their relationship with God. A "ministry focus," they argue, could be like Martha cooking dinner for Jesus instead of being like Mary who sat at his feet. This is certainly possible, but it need not be an either/or choice. If we are spending time loving others with real Christian love, but also depending on Jesus as we do so, we *are* abiding in him, as we have seen above. Jesus makes no distinction between Christ-centered service of others and abiding in the vine, as we saw in John 15.

As you grow spiritually, your fundamental life motivation begins to change. Instead of mainly desiring to receive, you will begin to feel the need (and the desire) to give. The experience of being loved by God transforms us as nothing else can. In a sense, the love of Christ spills over to others.

You still have needs of your own when you learn to focus on meeting others' needs. In fact, when you learn to give without looking for return, you will probably see your own needs being met to a high level. Those who focus on having their own needs met usually wind up dissatisfied. This is part of what Jesus meant in the riddle recorded in Luke 9:24: "For whoever wishes to save his life shall lose it, but whoever loses his life for my sake, he is the one who will save it."

When you look away from your own needs for Jesus' sake, you will find that you can trust him to meet your needs better than you ever could through selfish love-demanding. You'll become like Paul who always talked about other people's problems but rarely mentioned his own.

HAVE SOME DINNER

When his disciples brought him lunch after Jesus had been talking to the Samaritan woman, he said, "I have food that you do not know about… My food is to do the will of him who sent me, and to accomplish his work" (John 4:32-34). Jesus was being fed spiritually by bringing this woman to faith. We too can be fed this way. Nothing is healthier than applying our minds and creativity to the well-being of others, provided that we do so in dependence upon God and for the right motives. Paul says:

> Do nothing from selfishness or empty conceit, but with humility of mind let each of you regard one another as more important than himself; do not merely look out for your own personal interests, but also for the interests of others. Have this attitude in yourselves which was also in Christ Jesus, who, although He existed in the form of God, did not regard equality with God a thing to be grasped, but emptied Himself.
> (Philippians 2:3-7)

Here again, the Lord wants us to learn to think beyond our own needs and become concerned about meeting the needs of others, just like Jesus did.

Some Christians will argue at this point, "I know I should serve others, and I'm planning to do so, but right now I'm working through a lot of my own problems. How can I focus on other's problems when I'm still working through my own?"

When you're feeling an acute sense of need and hurt, it becomes more important than ever to deliberately get outside yourself, at least part of the time, to meet needs in others' lives. Nothing will help you keep your own problems in perspective, nothing will give you more motivation, and nothing will build your faith more than serving others in the name of Jesus.

Even in his hour of greatest need the night before his death Jesus took time to wash his disciples' feet. Afterward, he told them he had given them an example to follow. Then he said, "If you know these things, you are blessed if you do them" (John 13:17). To be blessed means to be enriched or happy, which we will be if we follow his example.

THE MOST-IGNORED MEANS OF GROWTH

In theological terms, this act of devoting yourself to the project of building relationships where you edify (or build up) others is called *ministry*. The word for ministry in the Bible is the same as the word for service. Whenever you move out in the name of Christ to practice serving love, you are a servant, or minister.

Today, Christian ministry is the most often ignored biblical means of growth. In recent decades, the western church has shown more interest in teaching members that ministry is important for everyone. However, they often don't view ministry as a true means of growth, like prayer or reading scripture. In major systematic theologies, serving love is not even mentioned in discussions of the means of grace.

Moreover, when modern teachers advance ministry as a good idea, they may trivialize it or leave its definition so vague that nothing happens. In one recent popular book on ministry, the author's example of "outreach" was an orderly who hummed hymns on the elevator as he took people to surgery!

Volunteering in a service ministry is nice, but ministry should also be part of the main stream of our lives. It's how we serve and relate to those around us, especially in the body of Christ.

Sometimes, ministry is not seen as a priority sometimes because of the division between clergy and laity taught in many churches. Under this teaching, average Christians do not view themselves as ministers, because ministry is a professional role, like dentistry or law. If your neighbor told you he had a toothache, you would hardly feel competent to take him to your basement shop and try to drill out his cavity, filling it with epoxy glue! This sort of problem calls for a professional; no lay person should ever try to do dentistry.

Many have come to view Christian ministry in the same light. They think the responsibility for ministry belongs to the pastor and church staff. Who am I to think I can help people with their problems? How could I build people up spiritually? Unfortunately, modern Christians have lost confidence in their own ability to do sophisticated Christian ministry.

But we can do these things, and if we fail to do so, we are missing out on one of the means of growth. No Christian who merely receives blessing from others will ever be spiritually healthy. Many Christians think their churches exist solely to meet their needs. How far this is from the biblical picture, where the church is there so we can meet others' needs!

Even though we may advance through the earliest stages of spiritual growth without developing ministry, we will not get very far. Failure to develop ministry is nothing less than a lack of love, and God declares that we cannot move ahead with him unless we develop meaningful ministry any more than we could do so without prayer.

Consider just a few of the passages that warn us that serving love is essential for spiritual growth:

PASSAGE	IMPLICATION
I TIMOTHY 1:5 But the goal of our instruction is love from a pure heart and a good conscience and a sincere faith.	If the goal of Paul's instruction is love and the other things mentioned, we would be failing to fulfill that goal apart from ministry.
EPHESIANS 4:15-16 Speaking the truth in love, we are to grow up in all aspects into Him, who is the head, even Christ, from whom the whole body, being fitted and held together by *that which every joint supplies*, according to the *proper working of each individual part*, causes the growth of the body for the building up of itself in love.	That which builds up the body of Christ is the power of Jesus being ministered to the members through every single member in that group, as the emphasized words show. Every-member ministry is assumed throughout the New Testament.
I JOHN 4:19-20 We love, because He first loved us. If someone says, "I love God," and hates his brother, he is a liar; for *the one who does not love his brother whom he has seen, cannot love God whom he has not seen.*	No one can develop true love for God, but not for others. A Hindu holy man might leave human society to find God through years of spiritual discipline, but a Christian could never do this. For us, growing in God means loving others. According to this passage, failure to love others is antithetical to loving God.
ACTS 20:35 In everything I showed you that by working hard in this manner you must help the weak and remember the words of the Lord Jesus, that He Himself said, "It is more blessed to give than to receive."	The word "blessed" means enriched. We have not experienced most of what God wants to give us in enrichment and spiritual growth if we only receive.

JOHN 13:34,17

A new commandment I give to you, that you love one another, even as I have loved you, that you also love one another.
If you know these things, you are blessed if you do them.

When Jesus says "these things," the context is his washing of his disciples' feet, which was a graphic demonstration of servant love. He promises that the one who practices servant love will be more "blessed" as a result, which implies that ministry is a means of growth.

LUKE 9:24

Whoever wishes to save his life shall lose it, but whoever loses his life for My sake, he is the one who will save it.

This directly opposes modern thinking. It means that those who live for self lose the very advantage they seek. We only end up being fulfilled when we deny ourselves through sacrificial love.

"I May Not Minister, But I Have the Other Means of Growth"

If I have four out of five means of growth, I may conclude that I will be 80% healthy. Not true. Because of the interaction of the means of growth, missing even one will eventually lead to a sickening distortion and breakdown of your entire Christian walk.

Because Christian ministry is so often ignored in North America, we have taken the extra step in this chapter of considering how the *absence* of this means of growth will affect the other means of growth. We could make a similar chart for each of the other means, and that might be a good idea for personal study.

WHEN A MEANS OF GROWTH IS ABSENT

MEANS OF GROWTH	EFFECT WHEN MINISTRY IS ABSENT
SCRIPTURE	People who have not developed personal ministry find it hard to see the reason for in-depth study of scripture. They study only for personal blessing, which eventually leads us to a strictly devotional approach to scripture. Seriously attacking critical issues seems like a waste of time to Christians lacking defined ministry, because they never have the experience of being caught without the answers in real ministry situations.
PRAYER	People lacking defined, regular ministry forfeit one of the most important forms of prayer: intercession. Instead of spending substantial time in intercessory prayer, as the New Testament authors did, prayer becomes merely a chance to build oneself up. Christians without ministry become increasingly self-centered in prayer, coming to see it as a way to be transported to another feeling state rather than a tool of spiritual warfare.
FELLOWSHIP	When a local church lives in the light of its mission and all the members see themselves as contributing to that mission, a healthy dynamic develops. Everyone in the church is looking for ways to serve the other members and new guests. When ministry is not seen as essential for every member, a different dynamic appears: everyone's eyes turn inward. When a church becomes inward-focused, in-fighting and dissatisfaction soon follow. Feeling states become the barometer of spirituality. People remain as immature as ever when they view Christianity as an opportunity for thrill-seeking instead of serving.

DISCIPLINE OF THE HOLY SPIRIT	We may actually avoid some discipline of the Holy Spirit by avoiding ministry. God wants to use our ministry as a tool of discipline in our lives. However, missing out on some of God's discipline in our lives is not a blessing, even though the carnal mentality might think so. Also, as we will see, a key outcome God seeks in discipline is to manifest the life of Christ in our outer persons. This outcome enhances our ministries. If we fail to develop ministry, we will miss this intended outcome of discipline.

FEEL THE JOY

When Jesus gave his instructions in John 15, he included the statement, "These things I have spoken to you, that my joy may be in you, and that your joy may be made full" (v. 11). Jesus knew that by loving others they would be fulfilling his command and receiving a blessing themselves at the same time.

Have you ever felt the thrill of the power of the Almighty God moving through *you* to *another* in an act of Christian ministry? If not, you may be missing one of the most important sources of enrichment for Christians. Jesus wasn't kidding when he said, "It is more blessed to give than to receive." The sense of reward is often tangible not only afterward, when the impact of what we have done gradually dawns on us, but even *during* times of serving love. You'll find yourself feeling the full joy of the Christian life as the power of God moves through you in this wonderful way.

HOW DO I START?

If you want to become more involved in Christian ministry but feel uncertain how to proceed, the following points may help.

First, before many of the best opportunities for ministry will be available to you, you must be "equipped" for ministry. This means you have to be trained to use the basic tools and skills involved in Christian ministry. It's your church's job to make training available to you. Paul says God gave the church leaders "for the equipping of the saints for the work of ministry, to the building up of the Body of Christ" (Ephesians 4:11-12).

Next, realize that establishing ministry is different than shining a pair of shoes. Most of us could shine some shoes with little actual training. We could also expect success on our first or second try. Three tries would definitely be adequate for all but the most incompetent.

Ministry, on the other hand, is one of the most complicated and sophisticated tasks imaginable. It also ranks high in value and significance. Those who hope to establish meaningful ministry based on a weekend seminar or a couple of attempts at leading a home Bible study are headed for failure. Personal ministry is such a valuable activity, both to ourselves and to others we should be prepared to undergo years of training and multiple failures, including some painful ones. There is nothing foolish about suffering intensely in the process of establishing a meaningful ministry. The learning curve definitely extends over years, not weeks.

Should you come before God and adjust your estimate of what it takes to establish ministry in his name? It's not for us to set limits on what we are prepared to undergo in order to become effective servants of God. When you set out on a course that is clearly the will of God, you should be willing to do whatever he thinks is necessary.

MINISTRY UNDER THE LEGALISTIC PARADIGM

Ministry is just as likely to become legalistic as any other part of the Christian life. When living under law, we take our identity from what we are doing. Applying this to ministry, all of us will find that at times we have fallen under the law paradigm with regard to ministry.

Taking our identity from our ministry results in a sickening perversion of God's plan. We derive precious boosts to our ego, or devastating personal deflation, depending on how things are going in our ministry. These bouts of pride or depression are not the normal healthy trials found in all sacrificial service; they go beyond what is healthy because we are overloading our service with a burden it was never meant to bear: our very identity.

Everyone feels bad when things go poorly in ministry. Even Jesus and Paul felt depressed about the negatives in their ministries. Jesus' exasperation was obvious when he cried out, "O unbelieving and perverted generation… How long shall I put up with you?" (Matthew 17:17). Paul says, after listing a devastating series of trials, "Apart from such external things, there is the daily pressure upon me of concern for all the churches. Who is weak without my being weak? Who is led into sin without my intense concern?" (2 Corinthians 11:28-29). He tells the Corinthians, "Out of much affliction and anguish of heart I wrote to you with many tears" (2 Corinthians 2:4). Surely Paul was depressed about ministry at times.

Anyone who serves others in the name of the Lord is going to encounter staggering negatives from the people he or she serves. Some of these negatives are so strong that they are bound to cause depression and an intense sense of failure at times.

It's also natural to sometimes feel "burned out" in ministry. Today, many seem to feel that something is broken if we feel exhausted from ministry work. But even Jesus felt exhausted (John 4:6). Like any kind of work, ministry can be tiring, and we need times of rest. But when we have been living under a legalistic understanding of ministry for some time, burnout takes the form of defection.

So the question becomes, when are weariness or bad feelings about failure a sign of legalistic thinking?

Weariness or discouragement over failure indicate legalistic thinking only when our depression causes us to become resentful or unfaithful to the Lord. When we quit or back off on ministry because of poor results, it suggests that we view success and appreciation from others as preconditions for ministry. In other words, we are not willing to serve if we can't have success and appreciation up to some inner standard of success and appreciation.

When Christians operating under the legalistic perspective meet with poor results, they don't change tactics or ministry fields; They simply walk off the job. But why should success or recognition be preconditions for going on? Isn't it because we are drawing so much of our identity from our ministry that we cannot tolerate failure without feeling like a nobody?

The dividing line is not always easy to detect, because results *are* important. When Paul spoke to the Corinthians about this area, he stressed that bringing in the harvest was exactly why he and Apollos came to Corinth. They were willing to cooperate with one another because the harvest mattered to God. Therefore he could say, "I planted, and Apollos watered, but God was causing the growth." But just because results were important didn't mean they were the basis for Paul's identity. He quickly adds, "So then neither the one who plants nor the one who waters is anything, but God who causes the growth" (1 Corinthians 3:6-7).

Paul's grace perspective was evident not only in his willingness to acknowledge God as the source of power for his ministry, but also in his willingness to cooperate with Apollos. The one who has a legalistic mentality competes with his fellow workers and seeks recognition from men for his work. Paul was unconcerned about how his success was being reckoned, and he was able to say, "Now he who plants and he who waters are one" (v. 8). For the fleshly Corinthians, however, he had to ask, "For since there is jealousy and strife among you, are you not fleshly, and are you not walking like mere men?" (v. 3).

Two features—the willingness to acknowledge God as the source of our power and the willingness to cooperate with others in humility—characterize the attitudes God is looking for. Any time you see the tendency in your own heart either to quit or to compete with other workers, you can assume you are beginning to slip into a works mentality in your Christian service. Anyone who has spent a long time in ministry has struggled with these temptations. Again, only the grace of God enables us to lay these attitudes aside and return to him with empty hands, asking him to supply us again with his perspective.

MINISTRY AND THE FAMILY

Our own families are an excellent setting for Christian ministry. A friend asked me whether my discipleship ministry was as strong as it used to be. I assured that him it was. I pointed out that not only was I working with the two men he knew about, but that I also had three promising young disciples (learners) at home.

If you are a parent, you need to realize that you will probably not get the chance to lead and disciple your kids when they are grown. Your chance is now, before you miss that chance. Your spouse also needs your love and ministry, especially because you are often able to meet needs in your spouse's life that no one else can.

As important as your ministry to your own family is, you also need to cultivate ministry opportunities outside your family. Some ask why we can't just minister to our own families. I would suggest two reasons why this is insufficient.

First, Jesus challenged us with the thought, "If you love those who love you, what reward have you? Do not even the tax-gatherers do the same?" (Matthew 5:46). Part of self-giving love is the willingness to go outside our comfort zone and initiate love with those who are not interested. Otherwise, the family and even the church can become *corporately selfish*. In this model, we may be giving to others, but by forming a circle and scratching one another's backs, we are, as a group, serving only ourselves.

This leads to a second reason why limiting ministry to serving our families is insufficient. When you try to lead and teach your kids, you do so by modeling the way of life you hope they will follow. Shouldn't your modeling include concern for people outside your home? If not, aren't you saying by your actions that your kids are the hub around which the wheel of life revolves?

If you devote yourself only to your children, you're demonstrating a values system that considers only your own children important. They look on and get the wrong message from this—namely, that they are the center of the universe. You may tell them otherwise, but remember, your disciples will usually do what you do, not what you say. You need to show your kids that you prioritize servant love toward outsiders without forgetting them. They will benefit most if your life is consistent with all that God teaches.

MINISTRY AND THE OTHER MEANS OF GROWTH

Like all the means of growth, ministry is an interactive part of the overall pattern of living God intends for us. We have already seen that the absence of ministry can distort the other means of growth in powerfully negative ways. Here, we consider how it will complement the other means of growth.

HOW DOES MINISTRY INTERACT WITH OTHER MEANS OF GROWTH?

SCRIPTURE   When others are looking to us for guidance and help in their walks with God, there will be a new urgency in our study of scripture. This is because, as discussed earlier, scripture holds the key to successful ministry. Feeding young believers the word of God is basic to most types of ministry. Even service-oriented ministry should be carried out in light of the Bible and should include the use of scripture. Active ministers come to understand the word of God in ways self-serving Christians never can.

FELLOWSHIP

The experience of living in a church where members have developed an others-centered perspective and a strong ministry ethic is truly one of the most edifying and exciting experiences possible. It is also one of the most difficult to find. Churches that adopt ministry for all as their ethos will equip their members and facilitate their ministry. They mobilize their manpower and financial resources to help people find ministry. A church like this becomes the natural place to bring guests and know that others there will not ruin your outreach or discipleship efforts, but enhance them.

PRAYER

Those who are strong in ministry know how many times ministry spurs them on to intense periods of prayer. People with ministry find it hard to imagine what it would be like to feel the obligation to pray while lacking the natural and healthy motivation created by ministry. Active ministers no longer pray merely because it's the right thing to do or because they hope they will feel better as a result. Instead, they have real tasks to accomplish in the lives of others through prayer. Those who are established in defined and personal ministry consistently demonstrate more appreciation for prayer than those who lack this vital means of growth.

DISCIPLINE OF THE HOLY SPIRIT

One of the main purposes of spiritual discipline is to make us more effective in ministry. At the same time, being in ministry will cause us to experience maximum benefit from discipline. We regularly find that those who are tied into extensive ministry are prepared and able to endure trials that conform them to the image of Christ for the sake of those who depend on their ministry. Those who are not active in ministry find it too easy to run away in the face of painful discipline.

TWELVE BASKETS

When Jesus had his disciples distribute the bread and fish to thousands in a miraculous demonstration of his power, they must have been amazed. One gospel says Jesus distributed the food himself (John 6:11); another says the disciples did it (Luke 9:16). But this is no contradiction. God meets the needs of people through human agency much of the time, and this is a tremendous opportunity for us to be a part of what God is doing.

The story has an interesting footnote. After everyone had eaten their fill, we read that the disciples gathered twelve baskets full of bread and fish. The baskets were twelve in number because they were the personal traveling packs used by the disciples themselves.

Jesus later interpreted this miracle symbolically (John 6:33-35). The bread was symbolic of himself, coming like manna to meet the needs of the human race. By participating in Jesus' work of providing a needed meal for the people, the disciples completed a picture of Christian ministry. Symbolically, they took of Christ and gave him to the people. While the people received a needed meal, the disciples unknowingly provided themselves with food for many meals to come.

But it would be easy to miss the key to this victory. The disciples could never have fed five thousand or more people with five loaves and two fish. What they could do was place the loaves and fish into Jesus' hands and follow His instructions from there. What they contributed was not *ability* but *availability*.

We, too, may sense our own inadequacy, but we can expect to be used by God if we offer ourselves to him for the task of feeding others in Jesus' name.

THE MEANS OF GROWTH: WORKS OR GIFTS?

In Romans 8 Paul teaches that we should set our minds on the things of the Spirit rather than the things of the flesh. But we also saw in chapter 7 that performance of religious works is not the key to growth. Is this a contradiction? Aren't prayer, Bible study, and ministry works? And if they are works, wouldn't it be fair to say that spiritual growth is based on works after all?

As we've seen, if we view them legalistically, these means of growth can indeed be considered works. Under the law paradigm, people recognize and promote each of the means of growth, but they twist them into matters of performance and duty. When we view the means of growth correctly, however, a different picture emerges.

We should not view the means of growth as works, but rather as actively receiving grace. Through the means of growth we reach out our hands to take the free gift of God's grace and power for spiritual growth. Perhaps an illustration will help.

Suppose you met an eccentric stranger on the street. For no apparent reason, he gives you what looks like a cashier's check for the incredible figure of $10 million. Although it looks authentic, you can't believe it would be. However, the check looks like it was drawn on a nearby bank. You decide a one-block walk is not too much effort to exert to find out the story.

As you present the check with a sheepish grin on your face and explain that you doubt its authenticity, you are stunned to see the teller look up and declare, "This check is legal tender!" Before she can change her mind, you order it cashed, endorse it, and stride home with a large suitcase full of money.

After word gets around, you throw a party to celebrate your amazing fortune. One of your friends stands munching a piece of cake and remarks, "Man, I can't believe you got all that money for doing nothing!"

Your head snaps up in surprise. "Wait a minute. That bank was clear down the street, and what about all that time I spent in line? What about the fact that I endorsed the check? I wouldn't have this money now if I hadn't pulled that pen out and done some serious work! I did quite a bit to get this money."

What is wrong with this picture? On one level, you did go to the bank and you had to accept the gift through a process of cooperation with the issuer. But is this "working for a living?" All you did was accept a free gift, and that doesn't deserve the label "work."

It's the same way with the means of growth. God has given us several ways to set our minds on the things of the Spirit. When we use these avenues, we are actively receiving grace from him. We are not really "working" as far as God is concerned.

Let's change our illustration a bit so it fits even better. Suppose that instead of receiving $10 million at once, you had to go down to the corner daily and meet the stranger to receive a $1,000 check. No matter how many times you go down, he always shows up and he's always good for a grand. Sometimes he even makes it $2,000.

You may ask, "How many times do I have to go down and meet him?" And the best answer would probably be, "How many checks do you want to receive?"

But even this picture is not perfect. Going down to a street corner and meeting strangers isn't anybody's idea of a good time. To really fit, we would have to devise a story where you received riches while doing something you enjoyed doing anyway.

So it is with the means of growth. Although some of us may not initially feel that reading the Bible or praying is fun, the more we do it, the more fun it becomes. Building good relationships and leading others to Christ would be richly rewarding even if they didn't draw us closer to God. The fact that God makes it possible for us to enjoy genuine accomplishment while also having our minds set on the things of the Spirit is a double blessing.

GOD'S PART AND OUR PART

With the means of growth, we are obligated to supply certain things from our side as humans, while God supplies the rest from his side. We must supply the willingness and desire to grow. We must decide that we want to know God more fully and that we want to become what he wants us to be. Also, we need to take advantage of the means of growth. At no point does scripture indicate that God will cause us to grow without the means of growth, or that he will force us to take advantage of these opportunities even if we don't want to. He expects us to come forward and willingly meet him through the means of growth.

The fact is that if we will not pray, we cannot expect spiritual growth. If we will not open our Bible, we cannot expect to attain spiritual maturity. The same goes for fellowship and serving others in love. Yet in spite of the fact that some things are required from our side, Paul is able to challenge the Galatians with the rhetorical question, "Having begun by the Spirit, are you now being perfected by the flesh?" (Galatians 3:3). We grow in grace, not by human effort, but by deciding to come to God through the avenues he has provided.

19
ONE LAST MEANS

God nourishes growth in the new spiritual life he implants within every
believer. But he wants to do more. After discussing how God builds up
our inner person in Romans 8:1-11, Paul turns to a second process we need
to undergo in order to be conformed to the image of Christ (verse 29). Verses
12-37 center on our attitudes when God allows trials to enter our lives.
To understand this part of the passage, a few simple drawings will help.

"Christ in you, the hope of glory."
(Colossians 1:27)

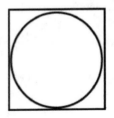

In this illustration, Jesus is pictured as a circle, and we are shown as a
square. Passages saying that Christ is "in us" could be illustrated as a
circle inside a square.

   But sometimes the picture is a little more complicated. For instance, in
John 15:4, Jesus says, "Abide in me, and I in you." This statement reflects

both Christ in us and us in him, and is similar to the statements we have been reading in Romans 5-8. It's not only that Christ is in us, but also that, according to our position, we are in Christ. The following illustration pictures both these truths.

"Abide in me…"
Position in Christ
How God views us

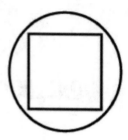

"…And I in you"
Condition
How people view us

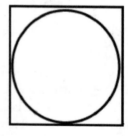

In this illustration, the top picture is our position in Christ. This is what Paul refers to in 1 Corinthians 1:30: "By [God's] doing, you are in Christ Jesus." The bottom picture our condition in this life. Just as God looks at us in our position in Christ, others view us in our condition. We also often view ourselves in our condition even though God wants us to view ourselves in our position, as he does.

These two ways of viewing believers also explain what has been called the "already-not yet" tension in the New Testament. Both are true of us, depending on how you want to look at it.

As we view ourselves in our position, the power of God is unleashed to build us up spiritually, and a gradual positive transformation begins.

A MODEL FOR SPIRITUAL GROWTH

Using these symbols let's imagine a visual depiction of spiritual growth. The next illustration represents the growing inner life in a new Christian, an adolescent Christian, and a mature Christian. The Spirit is coming to control more of the person's life as he or she matures spiritually.

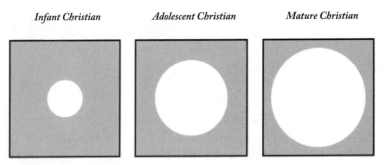

Infant Christian   *Adolescent Christian*   *Mature Christian*

But something is wrong with this picture. Although the inner person is growing, what's to be done with the outer person? My spiritual dimension may be growing closer to God, but my fleshly nature is still there.

A SECOND PROCESS

To deal with our flesh, God introduces a second process. This is a destructive process, often described in terms of progressive death. Paul says in Romans 8:13, "If you are living according to the flesh, you must die; but if by the Spirit you are putting to death the deeds of the body, you will live." This process of "putting to death" the deeds of the body is called the discipline of the Holy Spirit.

Our sinful nature inhibits God's ability to express himself through us. He wants to manifest the life of Jesus through and use us as instruments of his love for reaching others. To do this, he must find a way through what Paul calls our "outer man" (2 Corinthians 4:16), our "flesh," or our "mortal bodies" (Romans 8:11-13).

When Paul says, "If you are living according to the flesh, you must die," he is not threatening us with literal death if we sin. This "death" is metaphorical: the sense of misery and distance from God that pervades our lives when we live with a fleshly orientation. Notice that living according to the flesh in this passage is not referring to our life as non-Christians. The passage uses the present tense and describes, not conversion, but a process of spiritual growth when it says "putting to death the deeds of the flesh."

As God allows our old natures to be broken, the life of Christ within increasingly shows through. Paul uses the language of "life out of death" for this process. Just as we already died and rose with Christ in our position, here Paul says we are dying and rising as a process in this life. The difference is clear; our death with Christ is an accomplished fact, but this process of death is ongoing.

LIFE OUT OF DEATH

In one of the clearest passages on the life-out-of-death process, Paul describes it this way:

> [We are] always carrying about in the body the dying of Jesus, that the life of Jesus also may be manifested in our body. For we who live are constantly being delivered over to death for Jesus' sake, that the life of Jesus also may be manifested in our mortal flesh... Therefore we do not lose heart, but though our outer man is decaying, yet our inner man is being renewed day by day.
> (2 Corinthians 4:10-16)

According to this description, we need to cooperate with God in building up our inner spiritual life, while at the same time he goes to work on our outer person (the flesh nature), seeking to break its stranglehold on us. Paul says the outcome is that the "life of Jesus" can be "manifested in our bodies" (2 Corinthians 4:10).

To manifest means to show, reveal, or demonstrate. God wants to show himself through us, but something is preventing him. Our outer selves continue to project us, not Christ, to the watching world. If we want to manifest the life of Christ, we will have to submit to a painful but necessary process of gradual death in our outer persons.

In 2 Corinthians 4:12, Paul says "So death works in us, but life in you." Here is a key to effective Christian service, or ministry. When believers cooperate with God's work, they become more able to build up other believers. Have you ever wondered why some people generate such powerful blessing when they minister to us? It's usually more than just years of study and prayer. According to Paul, suffering in their lives allows them to worklife in others.

If you want to count for Jesus, you need to realize that this will only be possible if you are willing to bear in your body the dying of Jesus, just like Paul. True spiritual effectiveness in Christian ministry depends on our brokenness and conformity to the image of Christ.

WHAT BREAKS THE FLESH?

God uses scripture, prayer, fellowship, and ministry to build up the inner person. But these won't work on the outer person. According to 1 Corinthians 2:14, "A natural man does not accept the things of the Spirit of God; for they are foolishness to him, and he cannot understand them, because they are spiritually appraised."

This means you can read the Bible to your flesh nature all night without the slightest effect. The flesh may even learn how to pray and study the Bible, becoming a bold voice at prayer meetings. But spiritual things sail through the flesh without effect. Something else is needed to get at our flesh nature.

To break down the rule of our flesh nature, God uses outward experience and circumstances. Just as spiritual things affect the inner person, circumstances and outward things affect the flesh.

I can't stand living with these
roommates! I'm going to get married.

Wow, marriage is harder than I
thought it would be!

Affliction, illness, persecution, failure, or danger are like blows upon the hard shell of the flesh. Potentially, we could see a crack forged through the shell.

As these cracks widen, more and more of Christ is manifested through us:

BREAKING THE EARTHEN VESSEL

Paul uses some ominous language when discussing the Holy Spirit's breaking work. In Romans 8:36 he says, "For your sake, we are being put to death all day long." In another passage he says, "We are afflicted in every way, but not crushed; perplexed, but not despairing; persecuted, but not forsaken; struck down, but not destroyed" (2 Corinthians 4:8-9).

The heart of sin is self-sufficiency. God may use virtually any kind of suffering experience to strike blows at our self-sufficiency. As we face failure, suffering, and pain, we are thrown back into dependence upon God in a new way. Sometimes only the most acute despair will finally force us to abandon hope in ourselves. In 2 Corinthians 1:8-9, Paul recounts, "We were burdened excessively, beyond our strength, so that we despaired even of life; indeed, we had the sentence of death within ourselves in order that we should not trust in ourselves, but in God who raises the dead."

Part of the process before us, then, is unhinging our confidence in the fleshly strategies we have employed for coping with problems in our lives. If Paul's example in 2 Corinthians 1 is typical, only affliction that is excessive and "beyond our strength" (that is, our natural strength apart from God) will be sufficient to accomplish what God has in mind.

This description is ominous to the serious reader. But what choice do we have? Christians undergoing breaking either submit to God's plan for their lives or strike out on their own and devise a worse fate for ourselves. Clearly, Paul was glad he had gone through this experience, and no doubt we will be as well, if we endure it.

CONFORMED TO THE IMAGE OF CHRIST

In Romans 8 Paul discusses the big picture:

> And we know that God causes all things to work together for
> good to those who love God, to those who are called according
> to His purpose. For whom He foreknew, He also predestined to
> become conformed to the image of His Son, that He might be
> the first-born among many brethren. (vs. 28-29)

People like to quote part of this verse at funerals and other tragic events:
"All things work together for the good." In this form, it sounds like a
mindless, positive fatalism. But that isn't what the verse says. The verse
makes an important promise, but there are also important conditions and
restrictions on that promise.

First, God never says in this verse that he is the one who causes all
things. Rather, it says he "works all things together for good" under certain
circumstances. In a fallen world, God has plenty of suffering experiences to
choose from, and he need not *cause* such experiences in any direct sense. God
rebuked Job's friends in the Old Testament epic for claiming that God had
been the cause of Job's suffering, even arrogantly claiming they knew the
reason for Job's disaster. In fact, they knew almost nothing. The direct cause
of Job's suffering was the Devil, and their attempts to put God into a cause-
and-effect box were superstitious and cruel to Job.

Second, this verse does not claim that God works all things together for
good. It says he only works things together for the good of certain people—
namely, *those who love him and are called according to his purpose.* To those
people, and only to those people, everything will be used by God for good.

Finally, what "purpose" do we have to be called to, and what does it mean
to have things "work together for the good"? The next verse is clear: "to become conformed to the image of his Son." The connecting word "for" means
this verse continues the thought from the previous verse. God wants me to
become more Christ-like in this life, and when I am cooperating with that
purpose, he uses every circumstance in my life to further that purpose.

IS THIS ASCETICISM?

Many religious think suffering is good for stamping out the flesh, even to the point where they inflict serious punishment upon themselves. Some deprive themselves of normal pleasures. Others stab, cut, beat, and otherwise torment their bodies. These practitioners are usually lumped together under the term *ascetics*. Ascetics are people who think self-inflicted suffering is the key to spiritual growth or enlightenment.

Critics have argued that Paul was an ascetic, but he was not. Asceticism is alien to the Bible. Paul says these theories are based on human religious speculation and are worthless. For instance, in Colossians 2:20-23 he says:

> If you have died with Christ to the elementary principles of the
> world, why, as if you were living in the world, do you submit
> yourself to decrees, such as, "Do not handle, do not taste, do
> not touch!" (which all refer to things destined to perish with
> the using)—in accordance with the commandments and
> teachings of men? These are matters which have, to be sure,
> the appearance of wisdom in self-made religion and self-
> abasement and severe treatment of the body, but are of no
> value against fleshly indulgence.

You can see here that, according to Paul, things like abstinence from normal appetites and severe treatment of the body are worthless. Indeed, properly understood, these notions are themselves fleshly.

The verses we studied earlier about bearing the dying of Jesus in our flesh are completely different from the ascetic ideal. For one thing, we never intentionally inflict suffering upon ourselves. God is merely warning us that he will permit suffering to enter our lives. He is not instructing us to seek suffering.

Secondly, our suffering is not an end in itself, but a means to an end. When Paul says in one passage, "Therefore I run in such a way, as not without aim; I box in such a way, as not beating the air; but I buffet my body and make it my slave, lest possibly, after I have preached to others, I myself should be disqualified" (1 Corinthians 9:26-27), he is speaking in the context of athletic conditioning. His "buffeting his body" is metaphorical, referring to the kind of discipline athletes exercise when they train for their events. Just a few verses earlier he said, "For though I am free from all men, I have made myself a slave to all, that I might win the more" (1 Corinthians 9:19). You can see that his pain is not an end in itself. He wants to win more people to faith, and his suffering is therefore others-centered.

The emphasis in all biblical passages about suffering is not to seek it, as though it were a virtue, but rather to endure it in faith. We should never turn away from following God's will just because it may involve suffering. But neither should we be suspicious when God leads us into a period of ease or pleasure. God is not interested in seeing us suffer unless it's necessary for our growth. We can let him decide when that is the case.

SUFFERING UNDER THE LEGALISTIC PARADIGM

Legalists distort the biblical teaching on the Holy Spirit's discipline. Some turn to asceticism, and we have already seen why this has no place in biblical Christianity. However, legalists also turn to another, even more common distortion. They confuse discipline in love with justice, because they think you are being punished as you deserve. The following chart shows the difference between these two concepts.

JUSTICE	DISCIPLINE
Because of his justice, God will pay back evil with punishment that fits the crime. This is the doctrine of Hell. Likewise, justice rewards good.	Under discipline, there is no matching of given behavior with a corresponding punishment or reward. Instead, God acts only to benefit the recipient.
All human beings fall short of the minimum standard of good under God's justice. They are all deserving of judgment. Christians believe that judgment was carried out on Jesus at the cross.	Under discipline, the recipient is the object of love. Since the goal is the betterment of the recipient, discipline is related to needs in the person's life, not to acts of wrongdoing per se.
Justice looks to the past to ascertain whether the punishment fits the crime.	Discipline looks toward the future to determine whether the discipline will help the recipient improve.

Justice cannot refuse to punish one who deserves it.	Discipline is free to react in the way that will be beneficial. This could include doing nothing in some situations.
Justice would never act to punish one who has done no wrong.	Discipline may bring suffering into someone's life regardless of what he or she has done. Spiritual growth means breaking is necessary even when there have been no outstanding problems lately.

You can see from this chart that judgment and discipline are not the same or even similar. A proper understanding of discipline will lead us away from asking questions like, "Why is God punishing me?" While we would never want to rule out God's freedom to inflict discipline in connection with specific behaviors, the fact is that discipline is often not directly connected to a specific sin or group of sins. Instead, God is often working on our lives in a more general way.

The person who wonders whether God let his car break down as punishment for losing his temper is usually wrong-headed. This sort of speculation is related more to justice where God is giving you what you deserve.

Paul is aware of our tendency to interpret discipline legalistically. In Romans 8:33 he says, "Who will bring a charge against God's elect? God is the one who justifies." In the context of how suffering leads to spiritual growth, Paul reminds us to ignore such accusations.

Legalists have a hard time understanding discipline, because it's so *non-legalistic.* You see this when you observe legalistic thinkers interacting with the biblical call to discipline those we love. You commonly see two paradoxical reactions from legalistic thinkers when it comes to discipline.

On the one hand, they sometimes respond with a wooden harshness that insists that the punishment must fit the crime. They view leniency as a betrayal of God's standards. On the other hand, some legalists express horror at the idea of disciplining someone. They claim that if we discipline, we are rejecting or being unloving to the recipient. Ironically, both of these antithetical views flow from the same ideological font: legalism. They can't grasp how discipline could be neither rejection nor required punishment.

THE GRACE PERSPECTIVE

People who think God's discipline is always a cause and effect reaction to specific sins they have committed have their attention diverted to their actions as the key to avoiding divine "anger." Instead, they should be trying to understand what loving goals God is accomplishing by letting them encounter trials. Increasingly, those growing under the grace of God come to view his disciplining hand as a mark of his love and care. They are able to look toward God, trusting that he will work appropriately.

CONDITIONS FOR LIFE OUT OF DEATH

Not all suffering results in being conformed to the image of Christ. Some Christians suffer for years without significant spiritual growth. Instead, their suffering may only lead to bitterness and feeling sorry for themselves. If we want to grow through suffering, we must meet certain conditions.

CONDITION 1: ACTIVE, COOPERATIVE FAITH

God calls us to active, conscious cooperation as he transforms our lives. Passive assent is not enough. God wants you to step forward in a trusting attitude and seek to know what he is trying to teach you in each situation. You know you have the right attitude when you are able to thank God in the midst of trials. God says, "In everything give thanks" (1 Thessalonians 5:18). Notice, he doesn't say, "*For* everything give thanks." Some things are atrocities. Some things are tragic. We are not thankful for those things, as though God caused the atrocity. Instead, he says, "*In* everything give thanks." This means that even in the worst circumstance, God has a way to use it for your good, and therefore you have reason to rejoice.

When you trust in God's promises you can thank him for what you know will be the eventual outcome. Paul says, "All day long we were considered as sheep to be slaughtered. But in all these things we overwhelmingly conquer through Him who loved us" (Romans 8:36-37). This is the attitude God is seeking. When we are too spiritually blind to see his hand in our circumstances, we live in a world of fleshly resentment instead of spiritual thanksgiving.

CONDITION 2: SUFFERING NOT THE RESULT OF SIN

To state this condition more accurately and carefully: Our suffering should usually not be the result of personal sin on our part, including sins of omission. Peter warns us "By no means let any of you suffer as [an]... evildoer" (1 Peter 4:15). When Christians use heroin, they become addicted just like non-Christians. When they break the law, they go to jail. If you stick your hand in a fire, you'll get burned like anyone else. Any time our suffering is the direct result of something we are doing wrong, God calls on us to change what we are doing. Why passively thank God for a situation that is not his will?

For example, if you feel the pain of loneliness because you always come home from work and sit by yourself, God would have you rise up, go out to where other people are, and try to build relationships. You should not sit in loneliness waiting for God to transform you through it, because this pain is outside the will of God in the first place. God could use loneliness to raise the need level in your life, but unless you respond by acting, it won't have any positive effect.

God's grace is mysterious enough that it becomes impossible to declare with certainty what will happen in divine discipline. God is free to bless us even through suffering caused by our sin if he so chooses. Since grace is an undeserved gift, there are no conditions on our part that have to be fulfilled before God can bless us. But neither is God ever obligated to bless us, especially when we are doing something that is blocking his intended path in our lives.

Strangely, God sometimes does bless us through suffering we have brought on ourselves through sin—but not always. For instance, an alcoholic who refuses to take steps with his drinking will usually go for years without any spiritual growth. Yet if we are honest, we can admit that much of our suffering is connected in some way with personal sin on our part. In these cases God may use our own sin to bless us.

The Bible gives examples of this kind of blessing. For instance, God was not happy when the Israelites demanded a king. He said this was really a rejection of him as their king (1 Samuel 8:5-7). Yet he allowed them to do it, and eventually he declared that David's dynasty would culminate in the ultimate king: King Messiah. On another occasion, David committed adultery and murder in order to get Bathsheba as his wife. God disciplined him, but he also used Bathsheba to bring forth the line of the Messiah.

God can definitely bring good out of evil. However, he is not obligated to do so, and he may determine that the best response to sin in our lives is to let us "stew in our own juices" until we are sick of our ungodly way of life. This could be viewed as a form of corrective discipline—passive discipline, where God simply does nothing. But again, God declares that suffering should not be the result of our own sin. Therefore, we should try to avoid damaging sins of commission or omission.

Avoiding sin doesn't constitute spiritual growth, nor does it guarantee spiritual growth. Rather, we should avoid such things because:

1. It is the will of God, who loves us and has given himself up for us.
2. The consequences of sin in this life could be severe.
3. Many sins harm those we should bless.

This goes back to our earlier discussion of the common cold. There is nothing wrong with limiting the symptoms of a cold, even though doing so is not the same as finding a cure. While you are growing in the Lord, you should seek to limit serious sin, *even by outward constraints*, in order to avoid interfering with what God wants to do in your life.

CONDITION 3: NO ILLEGITIMATE PAIN REDUCERS

We all have ways to avoid pain. Maybe we withdraw to avoid relational pain, or we may drink or eat when we are depressed. Maybe we rage and shout when people get too close. Some run to another sex experience or spending spree when they're lonely. These strategies become a big problem when God is trying to work on our outer person.

Many of these strategies involve something overtly immoral, while others don't. Spending money or eating food is not a sin. But when these become illegitimate pain reducers, they are sinful and problematic. Our pain reduction strategies become, in essence, a ripcord we pull whenever our pain reaches a certain threshold.

If God brings us to a point of personal pain, it's for our good. But if every time he brings us to a point of pain, we jerk the ripcord just before his purpose is achieved, we effectively short-circuit God's work.

Teaching your child to ride a bike isn't easy. The child pedals around on training wheels for a few weeks and gains the feeling that he or she knows how to do it. But, of course, the child doesn't know how to balance the bike. Every time he loses balance, the training wheels save him from pain. To really learn to ride a bike, the child must take off the training wheels. Then you see him repeatedly fall and get hurt. The pain is temporary, and the long-term benefits are worth it.

You must be prepared to experience pain without the training wheels you have been using in your life. Otherwise, you'll never make it to the point where the dying of Jesus is manifested in your outer person. You must learn to do without the use of illegitimate pain reducers.

In Hebrews 12 God discusses losing composure when experiencing God's discipline:

Hebrews 12:11-13
All discipline for the moment seems not to be joyful, but sorrowful; yet to those who have been trained by it, afterwards it yields the peaceful fruit of righteousness. Therefore, strengthen the hands that are weak and the knees that are feeble, and make straight paths for your feet, so that the limb which is lame may not be put out of joint, but rather be healed.

Discipline is not enjoyable, but it works. The most interesting phrase in this passage is the last one. What does it mean when he says we should seek that, "the limb which is lame may not be put out of joint, but be healed"?

In the ancient world, breaking a bone could be a life-threatening experience. They knew how to set some broken bones and how to relocate some dislocated joints. However, they didn't know much about anesthesia. Imagine breaking your leg and facing the prospect of having an ancient doctor set that bone without any anesthesia!

Setting a bone is one of the most painful experiences known to humans. Yet, it was essential that one who had broken a bone hold still while the doctor worked. If the injured person thrashed about in pain, he could dislocate the fracture even more, possibly reaching a point where the doctor could no longer set the bone. Some people hobbled around the ancient world on crutches for life simply because they had broken a leg once.

It's no exaggeration to say that, in the ancient world, your future might depend on your ability to withstand the pain of setting a bone. This is the real-life circumstance that the author of Hebrews chose to illustrate our need to hold still and let God work. When he tells his readers to "make straight paths" for their feet, he is urging them to resist the temptation to flee from the disciplining hand of God into their artificial pain reducers. The stakes are very high. We have the opportunity to grow into authentic maturity in Christ, but that will happen only if we hold still and let the doctor work.

We dare not simply flee relationships when they get too painful. We dare not desert the role of service God has given us in the church every time we feel bad or fail to see the results we were looking for. If we won't hold still for God, we might effectively stall his work in our lives by fleeing every time he corners us.

A QUALIFICATION

You should reject *illegitimate* pain reducers. However, you need not turn away from *legitimate* means of reducing pain in your life. If you have a headache, you should feel free to take aspirin. If you're tired, you should feel free to sleep. If you're feeling stress, there's nothing wrong with a taking a vacation. Any refusal to use reasonable, non-sinful means available to us would suggest asceticism. It would suggest that we enjoy pain, or that we think pain is good in its own right.

Even changing our circumstances may be in order. If certain circumstances are intolerable, changing them may be the only wise solution. A lousy job may not be worth keeping, especially when a better job is available. A Christian wife with a drunk and violent husband who abuses her and the children should take strong measures to change her environment.

A legalistic mentality would insist we spell out which are legitimate and which are illegitimate pain reducers. But we know better than that. This is not a legalistic principle. God will have to show us when a given activity is becoming harmful to his plan for breaking our outer persons.

CONDITION 4: A POSITION-ORIENTED PERSPECTIVE

When Paul speaks of the life-out-of-death process, he refers to his own perspective when in the midst of trials.

> Therefore we do not lose heart, but though our outer man is decaying, yet our inner man is being renewed day by day. For momentary, light affliction is producing for us an eternal weight

of glory far beyond all comparison, *while we look not at the things
which are seen, but at the things which are not seen*; for the things
which are seen are temporal, but the things which are not seen
are eternal. (2 Corinthians 4:16-18 emphasis added)

Here we see what we should do while God works. Strangely, Paul seems
to say we should *look away* from the process of breaking even while we go
through it (just like we would look away while the doctor sets our broken
leg). He's teaching that we should look away from the breaking process and
toward our position in Christ.

Don't focus on whether your flesh has borne sufficiently the dying of
Jesus, or whether you are yet manifesting the life of Christ in proper measure.
Instead, look away from your condition altogether and focus on your position
(or new identity) in Christ. Trust him to complete the process of life out of
death, without constantly monitoring his progress.

If you constantly take your spiritual temperature, you become like a spiritual hypochondriac. You don't worry about whether you have a cold or some
other disease unless you notice some objective symptoms. If your focus is on
your physical health all the time, it takes away from your well-being. Some
people even become incapacitated by focusing on their ailments.

Likewise, in the spiritual realm, we need to set our minds on what we
already are in Christ (the unseen), not on what we have become so far in our
condition in this life (what is seen). If we sit around trying to measure our
growth, we will develop a performance-oriented perspective, and we already
saw the problems with that outlook.

Instead, look away from your current progress and move forward, focusing
on the things of the Spirit. In the midst of his discussion about God bringing
life out of death in our present lives in Romans 8 Paul says:

The Spirit Himself bears witness with our spirit that we are children of
God, and if children, heirs also, heirs of God and fellow heirs with Christ, if
indeed we suffer with Him in order that we may also be glorified with Him.
(Romans 8:16-17)

Why discuss our inheritance in the Kingdom of God in the middle of a
passage about spiritual growth and suffering? Because when we focus on our
future high status, we gain the courage and stability to withstand suffering
in this life. Notice how similar the next verse is to the one we saw earlier in
2 Corinthians 4:18. "For I consider that the sufferings of this present time
are not worthy to be compared with the glory that is to be revealed to us"
(Romans 8:18).

Only those who know where they are headed eternally welcome suffering. We have the security of future wealth and well-being, and that's a big part of why we are willing to suffer in this life for a time.

We need to look back to what Jesus has already done and ahead to what he is going to do before we be able to trust him now as he leads us through both pleasant and unpleasant experiences.

HOW IT ALL ADDS UP

Romans 8:29 promises Christians the opportunity to be conformed to the image of Christ. What does that mean? What would we be like if we underwent this growth process?

We have spoken of spiritual growth in the abstract and have analyzed its parts. Our study has also generally centered in the book of Romans—specifically chapters 5-8 and its parallels. But it may help to consider a real model of Christian living. The author of Romans knew what he was talking about. After many years of spiritual growth, Paul had become an excellent example of what God wants all of his people to become.

By far most the most detailed biographical material we have in the New Testament is on Paul. When Paul wrote the Prison Epistles (Ephesians, Philippians, Colossians, and Philemon), he had been a walking Christian for around thirty years. What sort of person is revealed in this literature?

To keep our study short, we will focus on the book of Philippians and refer to some of the other books when they bear on our subject in a special way. Philippians contains some of the most interesting material because Paul addressed it to one of his favorite groups, and he wrote it in the face of the gravest of trials.

THE SETTING

Paul wrote the book of Philippians during the two years mentioned at the end of Acts 28, after his arrest in Judea and transport to Rome for trial. Luke says, "When we got to Rome, Paul was allowed to live by himself, with a soldier to guard him" (Acts 28:16 NIV). We read in verses 30-31, "For two whole years Paul stayed there in his own rented house and welcomed all who came to see him. Boldly and without hindrance he preached the kingdom of God and taught about the Lord Jesus Christ."

From the first chapter of Philippians we see that Paul was facing possible death at the hands of the Romans. The charges against him often carried the death penalty, and his hearing with Caesar's court must have been imminent. Philippians 1:20-23 and 2:17 make it clear that Paul was contemplating the real possibility of his own death.

WHY IS THIS MAN IN JAIL?

At this time, Paul was probably the most competent and experienced Christian church planter in the world. It must have been terribly difficult for this man of action, training, and competence to understand God's reasons for leaving him in prison—first in Palestine for two years, and then in Rome for another two.

THE PALACE GUARD

Earlier we discussed the need to look at our problems from the perspective of what God is doing. This is the "vertical perspective." Paul had this perspective, as we clearly see in Philippians 1:12:

> Now I want you to know, brothers, that what has happened to me [his imprisonment] has really served to advance the gospel. As a result, it has become clear throughout the whole palace guard and to everyone else that I am in chains for Christ. (NIV)

Imagine Paul turning to God with the painful question of why he had been left in jail, only to look down to his manacled wrist. His eyes follow the chain until it ends—fastened to the wrist of his private Roman guard. A smile slowly spreads over Paul's face. "Hi!" he says, as he warms to another opportunity to share his faith. The Roman soldier chained to Paul's arm probably believed he had his prisoner securely locked in place. Meanwhile, Paul felt that the soldier was *his* prisoner!

The palace guard, or Praetorian Guard, refers to a Roman legion of around seven thousand men in Rome. They were an elite, very influential corps. Even if the term "entire palace guard" is hyperbole, it's a remarkable statement.

We know from studies of the early church that Christianity was spread in part by retiring soldiers. After their lengthy service to the state, soldiers could retire to a piece of land they were given in one of the provinces. There they became influential landed gentry. Who would have guessed that God would have Paul chained to men who had to listen to a complete, carefully reasoned presentation of the Gospel every day, and that this would spread Christianity throughout this elite group of Roman citizens, and from there, throughout the empire? Paul knew something we should remember: When suffering trials, God is often prepared to accomplish goals through us if we will only adopt the right point of view.

Paul was looking for God's purposes in his circumstances. He perfectly illustrates the vertical perspective—an attitude that looks at things from God's viewpoint rather than man's. I think this vertical attitude is the most striking thing about Paul in his later years.

Paul often goes so far as to call himself the prisoner of the Lord (Ephesians 3:1, 4:1; 2 Timothy 1:8, Philemon 1, 9). He no longer acknowledged humans as the ones holding him prisoner. If he was a prisoner (and, of course, the reason for his imprisonment was his witness for Christ, not any wrongdoing), it was because God had him there for his own purposes. With such an expectant faith, Paul was in position to make the most out of a situation that must have seemed absurd on the horizontal level.

THE PRISON EPISTLES AND THE CHURCH IN ROME

With scores of local churches yearning for a visit from Paul, not to mention his burden for reaching unreached areas like Spain (Romans 15:24-28), it must have been very difficult for Paul to set aside time to write. The importance of writing is rarely obvious to a man of action, or to those needing immediate help in their ministries. But God knows well how the written word can be used, and of course, this was no ordinary written material.

The young churches in the first century probably had no way of knowing that their sacrifice in losing access to Paul's gifted genius would result in the production of four marvelous epistles that have ministered to uncounted millions through twenty centuries. These books probably would not exist if

God had not allowed Paul to be imprisoned at the height of his career.

But that isn't all. He goes on to say, "Because of my chains, most of the brothers in the Lord have been encouraged to speak the word of God more courageously and fearlessly" (Philippians 1:14 NIV). Paul's example also galvanized action in the Christian community in Rome.

Neither of these positive outcomes would have happened if Paul had sat feeling sorry for himself. Those who look at life only on the horizontal axis see other people and events in control and cannot see the hand of God at work. The horizontal viewpoint is our natural outlook without Christ. Even after conversion, most of us spend far too much of our time looking at the world from a horizontal perspective.

If Paul had viewed his imprisonment on the horizontal level, he would have seen it as the handiwork of anti-Christian Jews and a corrupt and repressive Roman government. Instead of keen eyes for spiritual opportunity, he would have had eyes filled with resentment, bitterness, and mourning for his own misfortune.

PAUL BEFORE AND AFTER CHRIST

In the book of Acts we get a glimpse of Paul before he knew Christ. He first appears when Stephen confounded the men from the "Synagogue of the Freedmen." This was probably Paul's home synagogue. When the council dragged Stephen out of the city to be stoned, they laid their garments at the feet of a man named Saul, who later changed his name to Paul (Acts 7). Giving him their garments implied that Paul was the one who brought the complaint against Stephen.

Then, after Stephen's death, Luke records that Paul launched a ferocious persecution of Christians (Acts 8). Paul later admits that this persecution included not only arresting Christians, but also killing them (Acts 22:4).

What kind of man commits such atrocities? Clearly, Paul was a zealot, but not a reclusive or inward one. He was a crusading driver, a man of exceptional strength. He describes himself in one passage as exceeding his contemporaries in Judaism (Galatians 1:14). In Philippians he goes even further, saying:

> If anyone else has a mind to put confidence in the flesh, I have
> far more: circumcised on the eighth day, of the people of Israel,
> of the tribe of Benjamin, a Hebrew of Hebrews; in regard to the
> law, a Pharisee; as for zeal, persecuting the church; as for legalistic
> righteousness, faultless. (Philippians 3:4-6)

Here was a strong, rigorous man—trained, disciplined, and fierce.

After growing under the hand of God, we see new features in Paul's character. How positive, encouraging, and nurturing he is in the pages of Philippians! He discusses his concern for Epaphroditus' and the Philippians' feeling eloquently in 2:25-30. Notice the positive and warm in tone in his greeting to the Philippians: "For God is my witness, how I long for you all with the affection of Christ Jesus" (1:8). He calls them "my dear friends" (2:12) and includes other endearments. Paul was now capable of real compassion and caring love.

THE EXPECTED AND THE UNEXPECTED

Having lived as a Christian for nearly thirty years, Paul could perhaps be expected to become a nice person. He was caring and able to nurture others. Most people expect these character traits from mature Christians. The classic picture of Jesus carrying a lamb points to the gentle and caring aspect of Christ-like character. Jesus, who taught turning the other cheek and cared for children, must lead his followers into a life of deep caring.

But there is also the unexpected in Paul's character, even at this late date. Look at the language in chapter 3:2: "Beware of the dogs, beware of the evil workers, beware of the false circumcision." Is it possible that the apostle is calling fellow human beings "dogs?" Are we mistaken in the impression that he is labeling people as "evil workers?"

How could anyone, especially a Christian apostle, justify calling people such names? This seems more like the Paul who killed others before he knew Christ. Yet those of us who believe the scriptures are divinely inspired can hardly question whether it was ethical for Paul to speak this way. The fact is, God didn't remove Paul's toughness during the process of spiritual growth. Paul was still aggressive and tough when he needed to be, even after decades in the faith.

Here is a lesson for us: When God transforms the lives of believers he will not take away basic personality features. Instead, he will transform those features, giving us control over our questionable personality traits, while supplying new, complimentary traits—traits that fill in the blanks in our character. Not all Christians will become as aggressive as Paul. This man was so tough he could endure a list of persecutions that seems like a fanciful nightmare (2 Corinthians 11). The Philippians themselves had witnessed him being publicly beaten in their own city square, only to find him singing hymns and praising God later that evening in a dungeon! This was no ordinary man.

Paul's outrage in Philippians 3 is directed toward those who were trying to impose the law on Christian believers, and it is phenomenal. Earlier he even suggested that, as long as they had their knives out and sharpened, they ought to carry their zeal for circumcision to the logical conclusion and dismember themselves (Galatians 5:12)! We see a clear note of ribald humor here as well as outrage.

Again in this passage in Philippians, he calls his enemies the "false circumcision" (*katatome*) but calls himself and the other orthodox believers the "true circumcision" (*peritome*). Here the New American Standard Bible translators (unlike the New International Version translators) were too squeamish to frankly translate a rather profane and humorous comment.

Paul makes a word play on the word for circumcision (to cut around *peri*) calling his opponents those who cut—*kata*—off, or in pieces! This is a passionate, and actually rather funny, comment, which might earn him a visit to the board of elders in some of our churches today. Anyone who menaced the well-being of people in Paul's ministry was in for a fight. Here was someone who wasn't afraid to tell it like it is.

Even the Christians in Rome who were preaching for the wrong reasons are candidly denounced in Philippians 1 verses 15 and 17: "Some, to be sure, are preaching Christ even from envy and strife… out of selfish ambition, rather than from pure motives, thinking to cause me distress in my imprisonment." I think it would have been refreshing to relate to one who was this forthright, honest, and frank in his opinions (even though this is not what we expect of our Christian leaders today).

In a word, though Paul was a caring person, he was not a sissy. In Paul's character transformation we see that God kept Paul's fiber and strength and added compassion and the ability to care. Paul was still tough, even though he knew how to bear with the weak. Today, we don't always understand this kind of fusion. We too often expect the man of God to be a back-patting appeaser.

A MATURE CHRISTIAN WHO WAS FUNNY?

I am so happy that the Paul of these later years had not lost his sense of humor. In Titus, a book written even later in his life, he again lashes out at false teachers saying, "There are many rebellious men, empty talkers and deceivers, especially those of the circumcision, who must be silenced because they are upsetting whole families, teaching things they should not teach, for the sake of sordid gain" (Titus 1:10-11). This is not exactly a gentle analysis!

We could even consider this negative labeling! Today, we would send Paul to a course in political correctness. Apparently, Paul felt that those who were capable of destroying the spiritual health of young Christians didn't deserve gentle treatment.

But he's not done. He goes on in verse 12 to cite a Cretan playwright. "One of themselves, a prophet of their own, said, 'Cretans are always liars, evil beasts, lazy gluttons.'" This citation is surprising, but then he says something even more surprising: "This testimony is true. For this cause reprove them severely that they may be sound in the faith" (Titus 1:13).

How could Paul say this harsh testimony about Cretans (that they are always liars, evil beasts, lazy gluttons) was true? It's clearly an over-generalization, and rather profane. The answer is that Paul had a sense of humor. (I wonder whether he had premeditated the contradiction in saying that a Cretan [the playwright] was telling the truth when he said that Cretans are always liars?) If you don't smile as you read this passage, maybe you should loosen up a bit.

Paul must have had a colorful personality. And, if colorful, no doubt his personality was also winsome to non-Christians. A person who is strong, unafraid, and decisive, yet caring, friendly, and funny, would be ideal for reaching lost people with the love of Christ. Perhaps God would have some of us change our concept of what He wants us to become. His ideal for our lives might be far less dour and other-worldly than we think.

VERTICAL PERSPECTIVE: PRAYER DEPENDENCE

Paul shows an exceptional dependence on prayer in his later life. In Philippians 1:3-4 he says, "I thank my God in all my remembrance of you, always offering prayer with joy in my every prayer for you all" (also verse 9 and following). But interestingly, even as he ministers to their shortcomings through intercessory prayer, he remains thankful and joyful.

We noted earlier in the chapter on prayer that the hallmark of prayer under the grace paradigm is thanksgiving. Paul exemplifies how to pray about others' problems with the power of God in view. The book of Philippians contains ample evidence of conflict and disunity in Philippi, but Paul was not defeated by this knowledge. He could grapple realistically with problems while remaining aware of God's powerful hand. The result is thanksgiving.

He prescribes this outlook for the Philippians as well in the well-known passage we already studied in chapter 4:6: "Be anxious for nothing, but in everything by prayer and supplication with thanksgiving let your requests be made known to God." Philippians has been called the "epistle of joy" because Paul refers to joy and rejoicing so often in spite of his own dire situation and the problems in Philippi.

VERTICAL PERSPECTIVE: CONTENTMENT

Another manifestation of Paul's vertical perspective is his marvelous attitude of contentment. In what I consider one of the most important passages in the book, he says:

> I have learned to be content in whatever circumstances I am. I know how to get along with humble means, and I also know how to live in prosperity; in any and every circumstance I have learned the secret of being filled and going hungry, both of having abundance and suffering need. I can do all things through Him who strengthens me. (Philippians 4:11-13)

Wouldn't this be amazing? Imagine having the ability to be content in any and every circumstance! This is nothing less than complete victory over one's circumstances. If we just pretended we were content, this blessed state he describes still would not be ours. Only a deep-seated confidence in God based on years of dealing with him on the deepest level could lead to a perspective that was more or less always content.

The contentment Paul describes is not like the passivity of Eastern mysticism, which seeks to end all struggle against evil or pain. On the contrary, Paul has already said that he "press[es] on toward the goal for the prize of the upward call of God in Christ Jesus" (Philippians 3:14). The contentment Paul felt was neither complacency nor passivity. This is the kind of contentment that comes from a settled confidence in God's love and power. It was the certain understanding that God can use *all* phases of life for our good.

VERTICAL PERSPECTIVE: VALUES SYSTEM

Paul said God had completely overhauled his values system. Paul had been a Pharisee, and he was trained in Jerusalem by Gamaliel, the leading rabbi of his day in spite of the fact that he was from Tarsus, well outside the boundaries of Palestine. He was also born a Roman citizen. All these facts suggest that Paul was from a wealthy, influential family.

He apparently was a member of the Sanhedrin, which was the highest political office available to Jews at this time. His education was the very best available in the culture of his day. As a rabbi-Pharisee from Jerusalem, with money, political power, and Roman citizenship, Paul stood at the top of the social order of his day. He had it all.

After describing many of these benefits in his former life, he says in Philippians 3:7-8:

> But whatever things were gain to me, those things I have counted as loss for the sake of Christ. More than that, I count all things to be loss in view of the surpassing value of knowing Christ Jesus my Lord, for whom I have suffered the loss of all things, and count them but rubbish in order that I may gain Christ.

Like the person who has seen the foolishness in his obsession with collecting forks, Paul simply could not attach importance to the prestige values of his day. He had been transformed by the renewing of his mind, not conformed to the world system (Romans 12:2). A person with a vertical perspective like Paul's cannot continue to thirst for horizontal values like man-pleasing.

In the last letter Paul wrote, he admitted to his intimate friend Timothy, "I am already being poured out as a drink offering, and the time of my departure has come" (2 Timothy 4:6). This time, unlike when he wrote Philippians, Paul knew for sure that he had reached the end of his earthly life. Looking back, he was able to reveal how his values system worked:

> I have fought the good fight, I have finished the course, I have kept the faith; in the future there is laid up for me the crown of righteousness, which the Lord, the righteous Judge, will award to me on that day; and not only to me, but also to all who have loved His appearing. (2 Timothy 4:7-8)

To anyone who truly believes in the afterlife, a values system based on the temporal is sheer nonsense. Believers with the vertical perspective know that everything is going to be awesome not too long from now.

VERTICAL PERSPECTIVE: WILLINGNESS TO SUFFER

In place of his former quest for prestige, Paul now felt a willingness to suffer for the sake of spiritual transformation. He expresses this when he shares his desire, "that I may know Him, and the power of His resurrection and the fellowship of His sufferings, being conformed to His death; in order that I may attain to the resurrection from the dead" (Philippians 3:10-11).

Paul is not worried about failing to make it to Heaven. When he talks about "conformity to his death" and "attaining to the resurrection," he is referring to his desire to see his *condition* match his *position*. When Paul says he wants to "attain to the resurrection from the dead," he means *in this life*, not in the next.

This should be obvious from verse 12, where he says, "Not that I have already obtained it." If resurrection from the dead referred to going to Heaven, this statement would be ridiculous. He obviously couldn't have obtained Heaven because he is still alive! No, this is referring to the same thing he mentioned in passages like 2 Corinthians 4:11, where he describes himself as "constantly being delivered over to death for Jesus' sake, that the life of Jesus also may be manifested in our mortal flesh." Paul again demonstrates in the book of Philippians his readiness to undergo suffering if it means he will manifest more truly the life of Jesus to others.

VERTICAL PERSPECTIVE: EVANGELISTIC ZEAL

Paul never lost his evangelistic zeal, like so many older Christians do. We already saw in Philippians 1 that he was constantly witnessing to soldiers who guarded him. Of course Paul was a gifted evangelist, but his concern for evangelism did not grow out of his gifting. Rather, it grew directly out of his vertical perspective and his eternity-oriented values system. Because he knew God, his certainty about the afterlife was unshakable. This led directly to a deep-seated burden for the lost.

In another letter written at the same time as Philippians, Paul exhorts the Colossians to devote themselves to evangelistic prayer:

> And pray for us, too, that God may open a door for our message, so that we may proclaim the mystery of Christ, for which I am in chains. Pray that I may proclaim it clearly, as I should. (Colossians 4:3-6 NIV)

> Be wise in the way you act toward outsiders; make the most
> of every opportunity. Let your conversation be always full
> of grace, seasoned with salt, so that you may know how
> to answer everyone.

Remember, Paul made this statement while he was in prison. It seems that he
could never stop thinking about the lost. Because of his values system based
on the eternal perspective, Paul knew his life and the lives of other Christians
should be expended on the task of evangelism.

Calvinist theologians believe Paul held to unconditional election. But even
the strongest Calvinist knows that when God ordains the ends, he also ordains the means to those ends. One thing is clear: Nothing in Paul's theology
allowed him to become complacent about the ocean of lost people around
him. If we are to imitate Paul, our lives should also reflect this unceasing
burden for the lost. This friend of God was also the friend of the lost.

ONE OTHER FEATURE

The description of Paul's person and character as seen in Philippians and
other books written near the end of his life is challenging and attractive.
All Christians who thirst to be close to God look at Paul's life with envy and
perhaps frustration. But it would be a big mistake to miss one of the most
important autobiographical notes in this book.

In Philippians 3:12–14 Paul says:

> Not that I have already obtained it [conformity to Christ's death
> and resurrection], or have already become perfect, but I press on
> in order that I may lay hold of that for which also I was laid hold
> of by Christ Jesus. Brethren, I do not regard myself as having laid
> hold of it yet; but one thing I do: forgetting what lies behind and
> reaching forward to what lies ahead, I press on toward the goal
> for the prize of the upward call of God in Christ Jesus.

This is more like it. After three decades of the most intensive spiritual growth
and training, including personal bodily visits by Jesus and at least one tour of
Heaven (2 Corinthians 12:3-4), Paul still would not say he had it all together.
His progress was impressive, but he was still acutely aware of his own weak-
nesses. It is a sign of growth in grace when we become increasingly aware

of our unworthiness, sin, and failure, while at the same time also learning to trust God more fully. Clearly, it is possible to be aware of but not focused on our sin and failures.

WHAT SHOULD WE DO?

Why not do as Paul did? First, he says he forgets what lies behind. This means that in both the positive and the negative sense, the past can hold us down when we base our identity on it. Many Christians are plagued by defeat because they are constantly comparing their current experience to some golden period in the past when it seemed like they were closer to God. But Paul says he forgets what lies behind. The joys and victories we once experienced were for that time only. They are not for today. Now, God has a different path for us, and we should apply ourselves to finding and walking that path, not trying to relive something that is over.

So, too, with negative experiences. Some Christians can't break free from sins they committed in the past. I have counseled women who cannot look away from the time they had an abortion. Some men cannot forgive themselves for committing adultery. By accusing them, the Evil One is able to keep them in defeat for years because of their past sin. Still others cannot stop focusing on how they have been victimized by others. Past betrayals and evils can hold us back from what God wants us to experience if we cannot "forget what lies behind."

Modern therapists would probably charge Paul with being in some sort of denial for making this statement. But this is not denial. Paul knew what he had done. He knew he had murdered Christians. He knew he had been a powerful, wealthy man. He simply chose to relegate these things to where they belonged: the past. They could neither help him nor hinder him now that he was a new creature in Christ.

Instead of focusing on the past, he says he "reaches forward to what lies ahead." What is this? This is the vertical perspective! Paul looks to his identity in Christ, and to Christ himself.

Paul calls on us directly to follow the same path he did. In Philippians 3:15-16 he says, "Let us therefore, as many as are perfect [mature], have this attitude; and if in anything you have a different attitude, God will reveal that also to you; however, let us keep living by that same standard to which we have attained." What beautiful security and grace we see in this imperative. Paul calls us to adopt an attitude relative to the level we have attained so far. God is not going to ask us to do something we are not able to do.

On the other hand, if we stubbornly refuse to follow God by continuing to embrace negative attitudes, we have one of the most precious promises in the New Testament here: "God will reveal that also to you." Even when we are sometimes disobedient, we have the assurance that God is not going to forsake us. He will reveal our problematic attitudes to us. Then we will have the opportunity to repent from our hearts and follow him again.

It is to us today that Paul calls: "Brethren, join in following my example, and… walk according to the pattern you have in us" (Philippians 3:17).

APPENDIX 1: THE INDICATIVE AND IMPERATIVE MOODS[1]

The terms *indicative* and *imperative* refer to two verb moods the New Testament authors commonly use in their teaching on spiritual growth.[1]

WHAT IS A VERB MOOD?

The mood of a verb designates the verb's relationship to reality. Here, we are only concerned with two of the four moods in Greek:

A) Indicative – mood of certainty, actuality
B) Imperative – mood of command

The New Testament authors use indicative statements when discussing what God has done, is doing or will do. They use imperative statements when saying what we should do. In Chapter 7, we noted the specific relationship between these two moods in the area of spiritual growth—namely, what God commands us to do (the imperative) is always based upon what he has done, is doing, or will do (the indicatives).

God is signifying by this consistent pattern that spiritual growth depends on him, but also involves human volition and cooperation.

---

1. This Appendix is adapted from a paper I co-authored with my colleague, Gary DeLashmutt.

EXAMPLES

Romans 6:1-19 and 8:1-13 are two of the best examples of this relationship, but we have already covered them. Here are some others. In these passages, the imperative statements are <u>underlined</u>, while the indicative statements are *in italics.*

PHILIPPIANS 2:12B-13

...<u>work out your salvation with fear and trembling</u>, for *it is God who works in you* to will and to act according to his good purpose.

In this example, the imperative to work out our salvation is based on the fact that God is at work in us. The use of the word "for" indicates dependence or causality.

COLOSSIANS 3:1-17

Since, then, *you have been raised with Christ,* <u>set your hearts on things above</u>, where Christ is seated at the right hand of God. <u>Set your minds on things above</u>, not on earthly things. For *you died, and your life is now hidden with Christ in God.* When Christ, who is your life, appears, then *you also will appear with him* in glory. <u>Put to death</u>, therefore, <u>whatever belongs to your earthly nature</u>: sexual immorality, impurity, lust, evil desires and greed, which is idolatry. Because of these, *the wrath of God is coming.* You used to walk in these ways, in the life you once lived. But now <u>you must rid yourselves of all such things</u> as these: anger, rage, malice, slander, and filthy language from your lips. <u>Do not lie to each other</u>, since *you have taken off your old self* with its practices and *have put on the new self,* which *is being renewed* in knowledge in the image of its Creator. Here there is no Greek or Jew, circumcised or uncircumcised, barbarian, Scythian, slave or free, but *Christ is all, and is in all.* Therefore, as *God's chosen people, holy and dearly loved,* <u>clothe yourselves with compassion</u>, kindness, humility, gentleness and patience. <u>Bear with each other and forgive</u> whatever grievances you may have against one another. Forgive as *the Lord forgave you.* And over all these virtues <u>put on love</u>, which binds them all together in perfect unity. <u>Let the peace of Christ rule in your hearts</u>, since *as members of one body you were called to peace.* And <u>be thankful</u>. <u>Let the word of Christ dwell in you</u> richly as you <u>teach and admonish one another</u> with all wisdom, and as you <u>sing psalms, hymns and spiritual songs with gratitude in your hearts</u> to God. And whatever you do, whether in word or deed, <u>do it all</u>

in the name of the Lord Jesus, giving thanks to God the Father through him.

Again, by looking at the linkage between the statements (e.g. words like "since," "for," "as," and "because"), you will notice that the imperatives are dependent on indicative statements. When you consider the thought development in this passage you realize Paul is at pains to remind his readers of the basis for each instruction.

HEBREWS 10:19-25

Therefore, brothers, since *we have confidence to enter the Most Holy Place by the blood of Jesus*, by a new and living way opened for us through the curtain, that is, his body, and since *we have a great priest over the house of God*, let us draw near to God with a sincere heart in full assurance of faith, *having our hearts sprinkled to cleanse us from a guilty conscience and having our bodies washed with pure water.* Let us hold unswervingly to the hope we profess, for *he who promised is faithful.* And let us consider how we may spur one another on toward love and good deeds. Let us not give up meeting together, as some are in the habit of doing, but let us encourage one another—and all the more *as you see the Day approaching.*

In this passage, no fewer than five separate imperatives are tied to five wonderful indicatives. Notice the word "since" before the first two indicative statements, indicating that they provide the basis for the imperatives that follow.

EPHESIANS 4:32

Be kind and compassionate to one another, forgiving each other, just as in Christ *God forgave you.*

Again, it is because God has forgiven us that we should forgive others. Compare this to the statement in Matthew 6:14-15, where God's forgiveness is conditional on our forgiving others. The formulation in Matthew is typical of the Sermon on the Mount, which teaches the true nature of the law. There, the imperative is the *condition* for God's forgiveness, not a response to it.

DYNAMIC RELATIONSHIP

The New Testament also teaches that, although the imperatives are based upon the indicatives, in many cases the *experience* of the indicatives is dependent upon our willingness to respond by faith. In other words, if I fail to act in faith based on God's imperatives, I may not experience the reality of my position in Christ. Of course, my *position* is no less real depending on my actions, but I may not *experience* it in the way God wants me to.

Seeing this connection corrects a common misconception among Christians: that even after we have understood God's promises, we should wait until we experience God's power, forgiveness, etc. before we act on what He says. On the contrary, we often must act based on the indicatives before we actually sense or experience the truth. Thus, the biblical order is *not* LEARN—EXPERIENCE—ACT, but rather LEARN—ACT—EXPERIENCE. This also corrects the erroneous view that our response to God is not important in spiritual growth.

OTHER EXAMPLES

You may enjoy examining this relationship in the following passages:

John 13:17; Romans 6:15; 8:4-13; 12:1; Galatians 5:16-23;
1 Peter 2:2; 3:7; 1 John 3:14,18-19; James 1:21-24;
1 Peter 2:9-12; 2 Peter 1:3-9; 1 John. 4:19